Preparing to Teach

D0911705

What does it feel like to learn to teach? What experiences are you likely to encounter and what challenges might you face? This book gives you the chance to learn from the experiences of students who have just completed a course in preparing to teach. They offer all manner of insights, from the amusing to the cautionary to the thought-provoking. Course tutors provide additional commentary, identifying key themes and structuring chapters and the whole book to mirror the process of learning to teach.

Each chapter takes a different facet of learning to teach, the first exploring the motives and influences that lead people to commit to teaching. Further chapters concentrate on learning about teaching in the school setting, considering:

- the observation of experienced teachers
- interaction with pupils
- discussions with mentors and new colleagues
- the exploration of the concept of 'subject knowledge'
- learning as you teach, lesson-by-lesson.

Later chapters consider the many frameworks in which you will find yourself working, the Qualifying to Teach standards included, but also acknowledging tacit frameworks such as 'the hidden curriculum'. In the final chapter, students talk about what they learnt of themselves and how it felt to become a teacher for them.

If you are thinking of learning to teach, applying for a course or just starting one, you will find voices here that give you a sense of how it feels to work through that process. The book is a companion; its tone friendly, conversational, and relaxed. Even at the most testing times in a course, you can turn to *Preparing to Teach: Learning from Experience* and find voices that say 'yes, I've felt like that too'.

Jeff Battersby is Dean of the School of Education and Professional Development at the College of St Mark & St John.
John Gordon is at the University of East Anglia, UK.

Preparing to Teach

Learning from experience

Edited by
Jeff Battersby and John Gordon

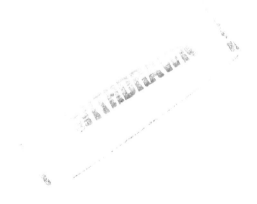

Routledge
Taylor & Francis Group

LONDON AND NEW YORK

First published 2006
by Routledge
2 Park Square, Milton Park, Abingdon Oxon OX14 4RN

Simultaneously published in the USA and Canada
by Routledge
270 Madison Ave, New York, NY 10016

*Routledge is an imprint of the Taylor & Francis Group, an Informa
business*

© 2006 Jeff Battersby and John Gordon, selection and editorial
matter; individual chapters, the contributors

Typeset in Sabon by Laserwords Private Limited, Chennai, India
Printed and bound in Great Britain by MPG Books Ltd, Bodmin

British Library Cataloguing in Publication Data
A catalogue record for this book is available
from the British Library

Library of Congress Cataloging-in-Publication Data
Battersby, Jeff.
   Preparing to teach : learning from experience / Jeff Battersby and John Gordon.
      p. cm.
   Includes bibliographical references and index.
   1. Teachers–Training of. 2. Teaching. I. Gordon, John, 1971– II. Title.
   LB1707.B38 2007
370.71′1–dc22

                                                                    2006015178

ISBN 10: 0–415–41584–5 (hbk)
ISBN 10: 0–415–30096–7 (pbk)
ISBN 10: 0–203–46401–X (ebk)
ISBN 13: 978–0–415–41584–2 (hbk)
ISBN 13: 978–0–415–30096–4 (pbk)
ISBN 13: 978–0–203–46401–4 (ebk)

Contents

Contributors

This book is authored by highly experienced teaching and research staff in the education centres at both the University of East Anglia and the College of St Mark & St John, Plymouth. The programmes at each institution are highly regarded by student teachers (evident in their evaluations), colleagues in partnership schools, and by OFSTED, which has frequently awarded their courses the highest of inspection grades. Many of the authors listed here have been involved in projects sponsored by the Training and Development Agency for Schools, developing teacher-education practice and resources at a national level, while some have also contributed to research informing national strategies in the secondary phase. All contributors have prior experience of teaching and management responsibilities in state secondary schools.

Marian Agombar is the Keswick Hall Trustees' Field Officer for Religious Education, working within the Keswick Hall Centre for Research and Development of Religious Education. She is the course tutor for the Secondary PGCE Religious Education course at the University of East Anglia as an honorary lecturer, as well as working across the three Anglican dioceses of East Anglia as field officer. She acts as an advisor on Religious Education to the Norwich Diocesan Board of Education, and is the Bishop's consultant on interfaith matters. As well as serving on the Standing Advisory Councils for religious education in Norfolk and Essex, she was Chair of the National Association of Standing Advisory Councils for Religious Education for a number of years. Her particular research focus is on the teachers' role and understanding in a changing Religious Education curriculum and the interface between personal beliefs and professional responsibilities.

Dr Roy Barton is a senior lecturer at the School of Education and Lifelong Learning, University of East Anglia. Prior to joining the university he had spent 18 years as a secondary school science teacher, much of this time as a Head of Physics in two comprehensive schools. For the past 15 years he has worked as an HEI (Higher Education Institution)-based tutor for a Secondary PGCE course. His research interests are centred around the use of ICT for teaching and learning, particularly in science education and in initial teacher education. He has produced publications in both areas of study.

Jeff Battersby is Dean of the School of Education and Professional Development, responsible for all ITT (Initial Teacher Training) and CPD (Continuing Professional Development) programmes at the College of St Mark & St John, Plymouth. Jeff was formerly the Director of Secondary ITT at UEA and lecturer in geography and environmental education, following 26 years teaching geography in secondary schools. He has had extensive experience in developing curriculum and assessment opportunities for pupils with QCA (Qualifications and Curriculum Authority), the GA (Geographical Association) and the WJEC (Welsh Joint Education Committee). He is also closely involved in research and development projects with the TDA (Training and Development Agency for Schools). Jeff has presented and published his research on pupil disaffection and on teacher training at national BERA (British Educational Research Association) and international conferences (Austria, Germany, Ethiopia, Malawi and Japan). He has published texts for teachers and for pupils, and his current research interests are in the democratisation of the classroom and ownership of knowledge.

Dr Nalini Boodhoo is a lecturer in education with responsibility for Modern Foreign Languages within the Secondary PGCE programme. She also contributes to PhD and MA programmes at the University of East Anglia. Before joining UEA she taught in secondary schools in Manchester, Sussex and Kent and has been a head of department, new teacher induction coordinator and a school governor. Her research interests lie within the areas of education in developing countries (especially school

effectiveness and school improvement initiatives in secondary schools), teacher education and foreign language education. She is currently engaged in research projects focussed on the development of foreign languages in the primary school curriculum and the learning experiences of international post-graduate students.

Sue Cramp is secondary curriculum tutor for Mathematics at the University of East Anglia, and previously acted as course director. Her many years' experience as Head of Mathematics involved providing continued professional development for members of her department, staff from other schools, newly qualified teachers and student teachers. Her current research involves the causes of disaffection in A-level Mathematics students and the continuing professional development of teachers.

John Gordon is a lecturer in education and course leader for English within the University of East Anglia's Secondary PGCE programme. He also contributes to the secondary course's professional development strand, Fast Track and MA QTS routes. He has authored and overseen the development of CD-ROM resources designed for training school-based mentors on behalf of the TDA, has completed reviews for the Teacher Training Resource Bank, and been part of a systematic review team concentrating on quality in initial teacher education. He has published articles in national (*English in Education*) and international (*The International Journal of Learning*) journals. His doctoral research has focussed on the teaching of poetry as an oral and aural medium. Previously he worked as a teacher of English and Media Studies in urban (and 'special measures') and rural comprehensive schools.

Dr Terry Haydn is a reader in education at the School of Education and Lifelong Learning, University of East Anglia. He worked as Head of History at an inner-city school in Manchester for many years before moving to the Institute of Education, University of London to work in teacher education. For several years he was the Director of the Secondary PGCE course at UEA, and is co-author of *Learning to Teach History in the Secondary School, Citizenship through Secondary History, History, ICT and Learning* and *Recruiting and Retaining Teachers*.

Dr Penny Lamb is the Co-Course Director for the University of East Anglia Secondary PGCE Partnership, and in charge of the

Secondary PGCE Physical Education course. Before moving into Initial Teacher Education, she taught and lectured in Physical Education and Sports Studies for 15 years across the state, independent and further education sectors in Dorset and Norfolk. Her doctorate research was centred on the ritual of excuse notes in Physical Education, and their influence on participation. Other research interests include issues relating to inclusion in Physical Education, and the training of specialist teachers to deliver Vocational Education.

Caroline Still is a lecturer in education and Co-Course Director of the University of East Anglia's Secondary PGCE course, co-ordinating the Fast Track programme. In addition, she holds particular responsibility for Science and specialist Biology training as part of the PGCE programme. She is involved in an environmental project working with Norfolk schools and businesses. Her main research interests are centred around Biological Education.

Acknowledgements

It is impossible for us to credit directly each quotation that you find in this book, given that many were provided in anonymous responses to paper-based questionnaires. Where names do appear in the main text, they have been changed to preserve anonymity of the speaker. However, we feel it is important to thank the many student teachers whose combined remarks constitute the substance of this book.

Below, then, is a list of all students who gained Qualified Teacher Status and the PGCE award in the summer of 2002, most of whom now continue work as fully qualified teachers. The experiences they describe typify those of many of the student teachers we have worked with, and we thank them all for their part in *Preparing to Teach: Learning from Experience*. In addition, we would like to acknowledge the influence of all students and colleagues we have worked with before and since the preparation of this book, whose comments and experiences have also shaped its content and ethos.

Johannes Ahrenfelt	Stephen Bell	Verity Challen
John Allen	Darren Bidle	Sarah Cleaver
Timothy Allwood	Aaron Blows	Timothy Cobby
Darren Armstrong	Michael Bone	Charlotte Cowles
Maria Arterton	Andrew Bonham	Rose Craig
Matthew Baker	Dorothy Bridges	Natalie Crowston
Helen Bannister	Sandra Bridgewater	Katie Darwin
Gemma Barnes	Severine Brinster	Rebecca Dawbarn
Juliet Beane	Joanna Buckton	Lorraine de Beaufort
Lee Beaumont	Nicola Burchell	Emma Dinsdale
Mark Becker	Daniel Carter	Shaun Douglas
Shona Bell	Ross Cater	Kaye Durant

Jihan El-Labany
Mary Ellen
John Etty
Sandra Evans
Thomas Evans
Iain Felton
Sarah Fenn
Simone Field
Katherine Fisher
Steven Fox
Jonathan Gent
Katarzyna Giaffreda
Christian Goude
Robert Gratton
Jessica Grindley
Tanya Gwilliam
Patricia Harding
Kieran Harris
Colin Harvey
Christopher
   Harwood
Richard Hawkes
Joanne Herald
Louise Hewitt
Paul Holmes
Matthew Howard
Christopher
   Humphries
Jill Hundleby
James Hurley
Massimiliano
   Imhoff
Daniel Jackson
Caroline Jeater
Gavin Judd
Nathalie Kausch
Andrew Kirk

Edward Land
Thomas Leverage
Claire Lunness
Aaron Male
Kelly Male
Penny Mancktelow
Lucia Martindale
Antony Mayers
Elaine McKinna
Simon Miller
Andrew Mills
Barry Mills
Guy Mortimer
Stephen Mortimer
Richard Moss
Beverley Murphy
Alice Neal
Janet Nesbitt
Keith Niemtus
Joanna Norfolk
Alison O'Donnell
Kathleen Ogden
Michelle Petersen
Steven Phaup
Esther Philpott
Tristan Philpott
Elizabeth Price
Tommy Rolfe
Lisa Ryans
Emma Scarffe
Johan Schutten
Jenny Scoggins
Hannah Seath
Ian Sexton
Benjamin Smith
Darren Smith
Edward Smith

Kate Southgate
David Spicer
Hannah Steed
Kim Steele-Atkinson
Claire Stephenson
Alan Stewart
Chanel Studd
Katherine Sutcliffe
Amanda Taylor
Elizabeth Tennyson
Sarah Tilley
Carmen Tomsett
Jennifer Tracey
Daniel Tregale
Emma Trimble
Joanne Tuck
Kevin Turburville
Alison Tusting
Benjamin Utting
Katie Vickers
Phillip Walker
Anthony Warren
Helen Waters
Andrea Wilkinson
Gareth Williams
Kate Williams
Kevin Williams
Michael Williams
Bridget Williamson
Louisa Wilson
Michele Witting
Ruth Woollard-
   Kingston
John Wrighton
Sarah Yates
Joanna Yorke

Introduction

John Gordon

About this book

If you've picked up this book, bought it or just browsing – flicking through in a library or book shop, perhaps – chances are you are considering a course of teacher preparation. Maybe you've just started one, in the throes of the first few days or weeks. In either case, you perhaps want to get a better sense of what lies ahead, learning from those who can, could, and did teach for the first time in a situation similar to the one in which you now find yourself.

You would have noticed that the book is called *Preparing to Teach: Learning from Experience*. But why that name? Even if you are only starting to think about learning to teach or the sort of course that might best suit you, you've already started to prepare. It's possible that you selected your first degree with this in mind; spent time during your own schooling on 'work experience', shadowing teachers with half a notion that you would like to be one too; or that you've made very deliberate steps already to make a shift from one career or profession to another.

We intend this book to be helpful at the earliest stages of preparation: to offer you the benefit of the experiences of others, of those already working through a course, and of those who have just completed. If you are just starting a course yourself, we hope the book can be a companion: that it describes thoughts and feelings you recognise, and at the same time offering some encouragement. Though on the one hand it is so much about communities and people, teaching can at times be quite an isolating experience: you may be the only adult in a room of youngsters, having little contact with other adults through a school day, even lacking the opportunity to meet with colleagues at break or lunchtime. If you are a student teacher this feeling may be exacerbated by virtue of your relatively transient 'guest' status, especially if you are the only person in such a position in your school. One of the most useful things we hope this book can do is reduce any sense in which you might feel alone, that you are the only person ever to have your challenges, problems or misgivings. There are the experiences of close to two hundred people represented here, often directly voiced. You should find amongst them some that match your own and, hopefully, some that offer reassurance, support or encouragement.

It is important to note that this book is not called 'How to Teach', or even '101 Tips for Beginning Teachers'. This is not really a book about *how* to teach, though of course the student teachers represented in these pages do offer advice at times, as do the experienced colleagues who worked with them. Instead, we hope it captures something of the feel or flavour of learning to teach across a whole course, the often challenging and very personal experience that involves. When we first had the idea for the book we were certainly very clear about one thing: that we didn't want to create a book that explains individual teaching competences, the minutiae of the curriculum, or ways of demonstrating each of the 'standards' (TTA, 2003) that every beginning teacher has to meet. As tutors, with combined experience of working with student teachers amounting to decades and involving hundreds of individuals, we were only too aware that the teaching profession already enjoys an abundance of books that offer such information, and that at the current time in particular, documentation telling you what to do and how to do it flows continuously from the Department for Education and Skills, as part of one strategy or another. It is easy in the face of such information – a plethora of frameworks, specifications and statistics, which of course have their uses – to lose sight of the individual, and of the fact that *being* a teacher – even more so the process of *becoming* a teacher – can be emotive, frustrating, testing and compelling. This personal, affective dimension is at least as significant as those that are codified and quantifiable: it is the dimension any preparing teacher lives – and it is worth acknowledging.

So most of this book is made up of direct quotations, drawn from student teachers, sometimes written and sometimes shared in discussion. The authors play an incidental role, making links between comments, highlighting contrasting views, or simply identifying patterns. Combined, the voices reflect on experience, and offer you a picture of preparing to teach informed by different perspectives, sometimes opposing but often in agreement. As such, the content does not fall readily into lists or bullet points, but we've done what we can to organise the book into meaningful chapters. However, teaching is usually a messy, open-ended business, so don't expect absolute coherence!

Context for the book

The student teachers who comment throughout the book constituted a cohort completing the University of East Anglia's secondary phase Post Graduate Certificate in Education. This PGCE course is the result of a partnership between local schools and the university's School of Education and Lifelong Learning, and individual course tutors based there are responsible for the chapters you will find here. In addition, the Dean of the School of Education and Professional Development at the College of St Mark and St John (Plymouth) also contributes a chapter and the book's conclusion, bringing to the text an alternative perspective. The authors represent a diverse range of subjects, and all of those offered by UEA at the time of research for this volume. These included History, Geography, Modern Foreign Languages, Religious Education, Physical Education, Mathematics, Biology, Chemistry, Physics and English: Leisure and Tourism has been offered since.

Of course, PGCE courses are only one of several possible routes into teaching, which now include those offered by Schools' Initial Teacher Training consortiums (SCITTs) and also Graduate Training Programmes (GTPs). Though the UEA course has its own distinct characteristics, it has many similarities not only with other PGCE courses but also with these other routes. Whatever route you choose or have already chosen, the experiences described here will often be relevant to you.

In common with most routes, the UEA course includes school-based placements and taught courses relating to subject specialisms and the wider professional role of teachers. Starting the course in mid- to late September with time observing in primary and secondary schools, student teachers then attend a taught course at UEA over seven weeks, visiting their placement school two or three days a week before starting a 'block' placement in mid-November, in school every day over a period of five or six weeks until Christmas. In January the cycle repeats itself, minus the initial observation and with an extended second placement, typically of a couple of months' duration.

Guide to content

Wanting to teach

The first chapter, Penny Lamb's 'Wanting to teach', explores the reasons that lie behind the very decision you may be about to make yourself: choosing to become a teacher. What influences shape such a decision, and who else might be involved? As a group, the student teachers Penny quotes reveal that the motives people have for joining teaching vary considerably, and that the decision to go into teaching can be made at very different junctures in their lives. Some students interviewed made the decision immediately after their first degrees, whilst others made a change much later on, often moving from a successful career in another profession.

Many of us can remember inspiring teachers from our own time as pupils, and the impact of these is clear upon many of the students speaking here. At the same time, though fortunately not so commonplace, is a reaction against poor teaching: remembered experiences of unhelpful and barely competent teachers have spurred some individuals on to represent their field of expertise more successfully, as if to undo the faults of predecessors. Also influential are family members: several of the students interviewed here, and on courses every year, come from 'teaching families'. Recollections of parents' verve and enthusiasm for their work are vivid, and a sense of the impact of teaching on domestic life is conveyed. Alongside the sheer energy and commitment there is often reference too to copious amounts of marking. The influence of parent-teachers was so great on one student that she used to 'play teacher' at home, having her own imaginary classes and pretend registers!

Before making the step to apply for courses of teacher preparation, many of these student teachers arranged visits to schools for observation. Sometimes they returned to their own schools, having to make a leap of the imagination from pupil-experience to teacher-perspective. In some cases, these observation visits helped individuals decide the age group with which they would feel most suited to working. Like some of them, you too may decide you want to become a secondary phase teacher because you feel that this is the stage of schooling where pupils make momentous decisions that shape their later lives, or perhaps you have a personal passion for your subject and feel you can inspire pupils just as you were inspired yourself.

A number of the students commenting in this chapter see teaching as a vocation and an opportunity to bring about change in the lives of individuals, with some viewing the choice to join the profession also as a rejection of a corporate, materialistic ethos in other lines of work. Penny complements the comments of students she interviewed herself with findings drawn from a survey of career-changers joining teaching (Priyadharshini and Robinson-Pant, 2003). The combined experience of students here suggests that they made carefully considered and informed choices about becoming teachers. Hopefully you will find remarks with which you can identify, comments that describe circumstances or aspirations that accord with your own.

Learning about teaching

Once you join a teaching course, how do you get to grips with its many different elements, practical and academic? Jeff Battersby's chapter charts the experiences of student teachers coming to terms with the myriad demands of teaching as they go into schools to adopt the teacher role for the first time. It's an overview of the whole process, considering how you might negotiate the challenges thrown your way and respond to the mass of advice you'll receive, which can often be contradictory. Which should you take on board, and which ignore?

What happens if your lesson goes so badly that you want to leave teaching, there and then, at that very moment? Worse still, how do you react if your mentor or tutor sees it? Can teaching really be so difficult? Many of the comments offered by students in this chapter reflect on how they dealt with pupils' (mis)behaviour and classroom management. Despite all the advice offered, and even though they knew what they *should* do, it appears mistakes are inevitable, in fact crucial, to your development as a teacher. The students here are candid, happy to describe their most disastrous moments. However, as Jeff points out, it is easy to be over-critical, missing successes and failing to acknowledge your own strengths as a developing teacher. Students also consider how they evaluated their own teaching, becoming willing to adapt to unpredictable circumstances, gaining the ability to respond positively to the most awkward situations. 'Expect the unexpected' is one lesson to be drawn here! No matter how well you 'know your stuff', no matter how good your preparation, the fact that you may be working with 30 individual pupils at any one time will soon make clear that not everybody perceives things in quite the way you do.

Learning about your subject

If the notion of 'subject knowledge' is not yet significant to you it soon will be, constituting as it does one of the three major areas of the Qualifying to Teach standards. Requirements specified by the Training and Development Agency for Schools (TDA) for all courses make it inevitable that you will at some point be asked to complete a 'subject knowledge audit', not only to identify your own areas of expertise and those for development, but also to assist those working with you, such as mentors and tutors, in giving you the opportunity to develop your subject knowledge as much as possible. This perhaps makes 'subject knowledge' sound simple and unproblematic, implying that there are clear domains of knowledge content within easily identifiable boundaries.

The experience of student teachers described here, and the con-textualising comments provided by Nalini Boodhoo, demonstrate that actually 'subject knowledge' is a complex concept, which no audit is ever likely to recognise sufficiently. The difficulties become apparent even at the point of application for a teacher preparation course. You may have encountered recommendations to demon-strate that 50 per cent or more of your first degree is directly relevant to your chosen specialist teaching subject. How, though, can any course supervisor or tutor be certain that your course is likely to provide you with the knowledge pertinent to qualifying to teach, given the diversity of university degree programmes, op-tional modules and different contexts for teaching experienced in those institutions? And what of transferable skills? Could you not argue that a graduate in any humanities subject may have devel-oped knowledge, skills and understanding relevant to several school subject disciplines? Of course, this line of thought already fails to recognise knowledge acquired in other contexts, perhaps profes-sionally or through leisure interests. And once you begin a course, no matter how much subject content you know, and no matter to what level, do you know what to do with it in a classroom, studio or playing field? Can you make it meaningful to pupils, appreciate their take on it, recognise steps in a thought process you'd like them to master?

Subject knowledge is so much more than your own grasp of particular factual details or your own ability relating to a particular skill: it relates to pupils' conceptions of subjects and topics, to the curriculum design of your subject, to methods and contexts of teaching, even to a philosophy of your subject, its values, aims and purpose. Furthermore, as the curricular as well as the 'real world' context continues to change, so must your knowledge and understanding of your subject. Certainly, it is not finite: your 'subject knowledge audit' may help you make steps forward, but you will never reach a point where you can sit back and say to yourself 'Ah, at last, I know it all now'. But that's perhaps one of the things that has attracted you to teaching, the prospect not only of helping pupils learn, but also of constantly learning yourself.

Learning through observing

One way of developing subject knowledge – in the more complex sense – is through observation, especially of the expert practice of experienced teachers. Sue Cramp asks student teachers about the benefits of observation, and about approaches they have taken to it. The chapter traces learning from the earliest observations – those made even before you decide you want to teach, during your time as a pupil – to those made late in a course after considerable experience of teaching classes yourself. As in the chapter 'Wanting to teach', it becomes clear what a powerful influence your own teachers may be on your own developing style in areas such as your relationship with pupils, your exposition during lessons, even your attitude to administrative responsibilities.

One of the challenges of observing once you begin a course is to move beyond observation from the pupil perspective towards consideration of the design of the whole lesson, and the way it might help all pupils learn. For some students, observing others helped them identify appropriate expectations of pupil behaviour: even though you may become aware of rules for behaviour in a given school, it can be especially useful to see how these operate in practice. The students commenting in this chapter identify progress they make from early observing preoccupied with the actions of the teacher, towards greater focus on the learning of pupils, at the same time commenting on how they learned to observe, a skill in itself. Increasingly, their observations were made with a specific purpose in mind. Sometimes they observed concentrating on a particular approach to a topic, or to reflect on how an experienced teacher arranged a lesson to allow all pupils across the ability range to be sufficiently supported and challenged. Others remark on observations they made in subject areas other than their own, and the insight this can provide. You too may find, as in the case of one student here, that observing yourself is an extremely powerful means of developing your teaching.

Learning about pupils

As well as watching colleagues teaching, you will probably learn a great deal during the time you spend working with pupils yourself. The chapter 'Learning about your subject' indicated that this involves a sensitivity not only to what pupils know, but also to their misconceptions. Pupils' level of understanding at any one time will become apparent in all sorts of different situations, at the point of whole-class discussion, eavesdropping on small group activities, watching pupils work in a gym or drama studio, or looking at written or graphic work away from lessons, in your time for assessment at school or at home.

As you work through placements you will gain not only a good understanding of what to expect of pupils generally at different stages in their education (depending on their year group, say, or key stage), but also of the way in which individuals respond to certain activities, the ways in which they think. As you see pupils working in your lessons over time, and perhaps in other subject areas through observation, you may develop a sense of their broader interests and motivations, the way they relate to other teachers and to each other. At some point it is inevitable too that a pupil will know something you do not, or that one possesses a skill or aptitude you don't have. How should you react? How do you learn from the experience to inform your teaching in future?

As well as learning about pupils through working closely with them, you will encounter during your periods in school diverse sources of information about each individual. Some of this will be confidential, relating to particular learning needs or circumstances which may affect an individual's response to your subject, to other people and to the experience of school. Other information available may derive from other schools and earlier examinations, from primary school perhaps, schools in other local authorities, or schools abroad. You will have access to files, reports, statements and mark books, gain information from parents, and learn a great deal too from informal comment from other teachers. One of the challenges you face as you prepare to teach is how to interpret all this information, and how to act on it to help each pupil learn. You will be working through a cycle very similar to the one your mentor works through with you.

Learning while teaching and with teachers

Roy Barton's chapter reports on students' thoughts on learning from the experience of working alongside experienced colleagues. Roy describes the nature of the student–mentor relationship, and students offer some suggestions on how to make the most of opportunities presented in such dialogue. Roy also outlines a cycle of formative assessment common to many courses, in which you meet with your mentor on a regular basis to reflect on achievements to date and then to agree on areas for development over the week to follow, often devising very precise targets to be reviewed at a later date. Some courses, like the one described here, use a form of log or journal to record the outcomes of these meetings. The chapter provides a very detailed account of just such a log and the way in which it recorded and informed progress over a placement.

Of course, meetings with your mentor are not the only way in which you learn from colleagues during your time in school. The role of observation has already been mentioned, and in addition there are numerous ways of being introduced to teaching responsibilities gradually, such as team-teaching. This may involve working with your mentor (or indeed another colleague) to take responsibility for leading a section of the lesson, introducing a particular activity or having a go at a teacher-led phase involving, perhaps, explanation and use of a whiteboard. The student teachers commenting in this chapter indicate that though this can be a very positive experience, it presents its own challenges! Of particular importance in this chapter are the comments students make not only about the good advice from mentors and colleagues, but also concerning how they responded to comments that were at first difficult to take. For many speaking here, the ability to be candid about your mistakes and openly acknowledge difficulties becomes key to learning about teaching and continuing to make good progress.

Learning from 'the hidden curriculum'

Moments of preparing to teach are likely to pull you up sharp, to force you to interrogate your own values and beliefs. You may gain a heightened awareness, for example, of the diversity of pupils' home backgrounds, where values and beliefs differ significantly from your own. Maybe your subject necessitates you dealing with controversial subjects, those that provoke impassioned debate and emotional response.

The students who comment in Marian Agombar's chapter describe the points at which they became aware of 'the hidden curriculum' – those aspects of education that are not easily contained in subject curricula and other written documents, yet which may constitute the most powerful basis for learning about life in the school experience of a pupil.

Have you ever considered the power of teachers as role models? Is it possible that the way you respond to pupils, for instance in the way you treat comments from boys and girls, reinforces certain stereotypes about the sexes? Does your teaching style perpetuate stereotyped behaviour in itself? Frequently these questions do not remain hypothetical, abstruse contemplation: they arise from memorable moments of teaching, presenting personal challenges to student teachers. Even the most innocuous item – remaining unseen – causes one student to reconsider. Who would have thought a belly-button ring could create such a seminal moment? At the same time, students describe moments when they have made crucial decisions about the welfare of children in their care, the full implications of the phrase *in loco parentis* coming to be recognised.

Running throughout the chapter is a sense of students rethinking their view of teaching, returning to their motives for joining the profession, and often redefining their understanding of education.

Learning to work within frameworks

As you begin to teach you will find yourself engaging with a variety of frameworks, from the institutional (your school, your course provider) and curricular (the National Curriculum, the Secondary Strategy, examination specifications) to the conceptual (theories of learning, subject pedagogies). As a student teacher you will have to familiarise yourself not only with these but also with the Qualifying to Teach standards. This framework specifies the knowledge, skills and understanding you must demonstrate during your course, and as such represents a framework for assessment. However, it has no doubt influenced the structure of the course you follow significantly too, making it to a greater or lesser extent a framework for your learning also, shaping decisions about the sequence of your course programme, the nature of activities in each session, or the emphasis of course assignments.

Terry Haydn's chapter identifies a number of the frameworks you will encounter and their relationships, while students describe their experiences of working within them. Terry also includes the comments of school-based mentors and university tutors, the various perspectives teasing out the implications of frameworks for your daily life as a student teacher. It becomes very clear that no teacher can act as a completely 'free agent'. Part of becoming a successful teacher seems to be about understanding these frameworks, recognising that sometimes their aims and values may contradict each other.

The remarks made by students could be helpful to you in the way that they offer advice about how to respond to so many frameworks, many describing moments when they realised that it is not absolutely necessary to know every detail of every framework from the start, that some details are more significant than others, and that frameworks which exist in document form often need some mediating to be understood in practice, requiring some adjustment to the necessities of time, place or people involved.

The remarks made by mentors and tutors highlight the importance of your professionalism (itself 'frameworked' in area one of the Qualifying to Teach standards) in schools and the other contexts for your learning during your course, acknowledging too that not all frameworks are explicit or codified. Schools but also individual departments have their own – often unspoken – value systems which inform professional relationships, interaction with pupils, teaching styles and schemes of work, and these can be incredibly difficult for you to gauge correctly in order to fit in.

Having successfully negotiated these frameworks in one school, you are likely to find strikingly or subtly different ones in a second placement. The combined experience of students, mentors and tutors suggests that beginning in a second school can be more challenging than starting in the first: you may have become institutionalised more quickly than you realise, the experience of teaching in a second school making the unspoken frameworks of the first more apparent, perhaps too bringing to light assumptions about teaching and learning you never knew you had – revealing your own personal framework.

Learning about yourself

The penultimate chapter is about how student teachers learn about themselves as they follow a course in preparing to teach. For much of the time you will be thinking so much about the learning of others that it may be difficult to find the opportunity to reflect on how much you learn yourself as part of the process.

For many students, teaching their subject to others makes them feel they understand it far better than they ever did as a pupil, even than they did as an undergraduate. The emphasis of comments here, though, is not really on learning in your subject. It's more about the personal dimension of teaching, about how becoming a teacher *feels* as you work through a course, from early experiences such as your first lesson, to moments when you feel your view of yourself in the role of teacher shifts significantly.

As in 'Learning about frameworks', the notion of professionalism becomes important. Many of the remarks in this chapter concern responses to adopting the identity of a teacher, and the extent to which that corresponds to the person you see as 'yourself'. Some students are committed to the idea that you cannot teach without acting, while just as many are convinced that you cannot be anything other than yourself. It becomes evident that the experience is different for everyone, and each student has their own strategy for becoming a teacher.

As well as contemplating your own responses to your development as a teacher, you are bound to receive commentary from others, often uninvited! Sometimes pupils may comment, but so too may friends and family. As you become a teacher yourself, you may have similar experiences to the students commenting here, whose close relatives saw them changing, growing in confidence and assertiveness, drawing on aptitudes and talents latent until teaching made them apparent not just in school but also in life beyond. Many of the students who comment in this book joined teaching because they wanted to bring about change. It seems that that process of change begins with yourself.

Learning from experience

The book concludes with a summary by Jeff Battersby, in which he identifies patterns emerging from previous chapters. He signals the significant challenges you will encounter during teacher preparation, raising important questions to have in mind as you work through a course towards Qualified Teacher Status. The same questions are likely to be ones you return to again and again during what we hope will be the successful and fulfilling teaching career that follows.

Terminology used throughout this book

Teaching has its own jargon and more than its fair share of acronyms that can be bewildering to the newcomer or outsider, so here we clarify the use of a few common terms throughout the book.

Student teachers

We have chosen to refer to those preparing to teach as 'student teachers' or 'students', rather than trainees. This accords with the philosophy of the book: that learning to teach is not just about the practical skills developing as a result of training, it can also involve education in a broader sense. Some teacher preparation courses are presented as Initial Teacher Education (ITE) rather than Initial Teacher Training (ITT), containing distinctive emphasis on the philosophy, psychology and history of education, as well as the specific 'competences' described in the Qualifying to Teach standards. You may encounter some confusion on the part of others yourself – maybe friends and even colleagues will refer to you using both 'trainee' and 'student teacher'. Where you find 'student' in this book, infer 'student teacher'.

Pupils

If we use the term 'student' to refer to nascent teachers, we can't use it without confusion to refer to the children they may teach in school. All children referred to are therefore considered 'pupils'.

Teacher preparation courses

If you have made any progress along the lines of considering a course of teacher preparation, you have probably encountered a confusing array of options. We use the term 'teacher preparation' to refer to all of these possibilities, which include long-established routes such as PGCE (Post Graduate Certificate in Education) courses, Bachelor of Education degrees (of varying duration), and newer routes such as Graduate Training Programmes (GTPs) and those provided by SCITT (Schools' Initial Teacher Training) consortiums. It's worth bearing in mind that the experiences represented here are those of PGCE students, though there remain significant areas of commonality with the experiences of students following different paths. There now exist pre-preparation courses too, such as the Students' Associate Scheme, while some institutions also offer 'booster' courses for prospective student teachers to brush up on their subject knowledge relative to the National Curriculum. It would be stretching our term's usefulness to include those, but many of the experiences described here will be of interest to anybody who has gone that far in preparing to teach.

The Qualifying to Teach standards (QtT)

All providers of teacher preparation courses must give students the opportunity to meet the Qualifying to Teach standards (2002) – sometimes abbreviated to QtT – and their courses are structured accordingly. Elsewhere, you may find these referred to as the '02/02 [February 2002] Standards', 'the QTS [Qualified Teacher Status] Standards', or simply 'the Standards'. There are numerous prior versions, and it's not unfeasible that you will encounter material relating to some of these, especially the '4/98 Standards', introduced in April 1998. Fortunately for you, the manner in which such standards are articulated has become rather less complex since then.

Training and Development Agency for Schools (TDA), formerly the Teacher Training Agency (TTA)

The TDA is an executive and non-departmental public body of the Department of Education and Skills, with its board appointed by the related Secretary of State. The TDA website (accessed March

2006) describes its own remit as working 'to improve the training and development of the whole school workforce. Together with our partners, we will help all school staff, teachers and school leaders realise their potential.' Part of this remit relates to your experience of learning to teach, because a good part of your teacher preparation will occur in the context of frameworks and initiatives originating from TDA. The change in the body's title is a result of an expansion of their role to cater more fully for the continuing professional development of teachers and teaching staff, going beyond its prior focus on initial teacher education.

And before you begin . . .

A good way to read this book, perhaps, is to think carefully about some of the comments from students in isolation, linking them to your own experience of learning to teach. Of course, only you can know how you respond to your own circumstances, how you are responding to the process of preparing to teach: each quotation will have a different resonance for each individual.

Maybe the voices here will confirm to you that you do want to become a teacher, helping you towards the decision. If you are already working through a course, they should provide some solace, help and encouragement.

No matter how the process of preparing and learning to teach goes for you, we wish you the best, and hope the experience shared by voices here helps you along the way.

Chapter 1

Wanting to teach

Penny Lamb

This chapter examines common motives people have for wanting to teach, and describes how student teachers arrived at their decisions to join a course of teacher preparation. The influences and factors are diverse, from parental role models to disillusionment with other careers. The chapter not only presents the experience of student teachers, it also draws on recent research into why people choose to make a change from another profession to teaching.

Training to become a teacher is not so much an apprenticeship as a journey of personal development, in which skills such as classroom management develop alongside an emerging understanding of the teaching and learning process. Learning to *become* a teacher, and all that this entails – being the sort of person who can command the respect and interest of children and facilitate their learning – is a very different phenomenon to that of learning *about* teaching, the genre many of us are most familiar with.

The process itself is ostensibly a practical one, though steeped in both theoretical and indeed moral justification. Courses of teacher preparation combine practical experience, personal reflection and theoretical rationale, creating an understanding of how youngsters learn to underpin classroom practice and contributions to whole-school communities.

This chapter explores the factors that may inspire individuals to want to teach, and the decision-making processes guiding people into realising that they want to learn about learning. Some of the thought processes experienced by students on a PGCE programme will be shared, representing a wide range of subject areas, and highlighting the often complicated and not so straightforward reasons and experiences which contribute towards making the decision to apply for a course of teacher preparation. The vignettes will trace personal journeys, sharing with you the factors that have influenced the decision-making involved in the application process. Such narratives also reinforce the fact that many individuals still want to return to an institution of education that years earlier they had so eagerly wanted to leave. 'Almost all intending teachers will have had much experience of being taught as pupils in a school. Without doubt, this will be the single most important influence on their knowledge about teaching' (Kyriacou, 1995: 9). This perception is endorsed by a PGCE Mathematics student, who commented that everyone has preconceptions about teaching:

> 'Everyone's an expert at teaching because they've gone through at least twelve years of education so everyone knows exactly the best way.'

Kyriacou (1995) reiterates that the experience of being taught certainly provides a broad framework for thinking about how to teach, but once the teacher's role is taken on, it becomes very evident that a whole range of teaching skills needs to be developed. These personal anecdotes and reflections, often diverse and far ranging, all appear to share common features, such as motivation and a desire to be a part of the education process. You may find that you relate to such experiences and reflections, or you may find reassurance or even some answers to questions you have as you read about other people's aspirations, dilemmas and, sometimes, even struggles. 'Like father like son' is a colloquialism, and when it comes to discussing one's chosen career choice our destiny may already be decided for us, for example taking over the family business and following in our parents' footsteps. Such a scenario certainly appears to be a strong pull to the profession for some students, as the following history student's comment demonstrates:

> 'I am here now partly because my father is a teacher and I had an idea of the lifestyle.'

Similarly, the experience of a science student:

> 'My mother was a teacher so I think that planted the seed. I had imaginary classes and pretend registers for many years! I have always been good at explaining things, and helping friends out with exam revision at university often brought the response "you are a great teacher", so that was a big incentive to follow the dream.'

The family influence is further reinforced by another history student:

> 'I have four teachers in the family who enjoy teaching and who would talk to me about it – this made me think that I might enjoy it.'

One student mentioned the support of his teaching parents when making his career choice:

> 'My parents warned me of the pressures that teachers face on a daily basis, but remained supportive of whatever decision I made. After talking to people in a range of professions, I realise everything has positives and negatives and that teaching will provide me with more positives than any other career.'

Likewise, another student stated:

> 'With having teachers as parents and being a close family, it was inevitable that my parents would influence my decision to become a teacher. The fact that my brother, uncle, both aunties and two cousins are also teachers probably had an influence too. Christmas-time is like a teaching conference.'

Such a background can, though, work in reverse, as the student went on to say:

> 'There was always a desire to be a PE teacher, but a part of me wanted to break from the family tradition and do something different. However, when you are sport orientated there are very few jobs that will give you the satisfaction that PE teaching can provide.'

A Mathematics student offered a slightly different angle on the family influence:

> *'At school if anyone had said you would be a teacher, I'd have said no because my mother was at the time and there were connections all the way through – three aunts, uncle, cousin, wife, so it's really in the family. And because of that I think I was nearly scared off but could sympathise with it. And when I was put into a pool of teachers and discussed it they were amazed I could put up with all their whining – for want of a better word! – because essentially there is a lot of pressure a lot of people do not understand. They think you just stand up and talk, get great holidays, get paid well for it and it's a walk in the park. Whereas, having been brought up in it, having watched my wife go through the PGCE course and her NQT year and starting to find her purpose in school, I knew that it wasn't a walk in the park and it's not an easy option.'*

This stance is also supported by a History student's version of how he came to choose teaching:

> *'Almost everyone told me not to do it! A persistent nag in the back of my mind kept bringing me back to the idea. It's a cliché but it has been something I've always wanted to do, however disguised it has been at various stages of my life.'*

Finding out about teaching

Being brought up in a household of teachers does appear to impact on the decision for some individuals to continue in others' footsteps. However, for those of us without the insider information, the starting point is to actually research what the job entails, and what it is all about, as demonstrated by a Mathematics student:

> *'I did a lot of talking to friends in the profession so I knew what to expect.'*

and reiterated by a student learning to teach Religious Education:

> *'I spent some time observing in a secondary school so as to get a real picture of the job. This was what convinced me that*

this was the job for me. I shadowed the physical education (PE) teacher and helped out in lessons. It was real "hands on" straight away and it just came naturally. I also went into a primary school so I could decide which age range I wanted to work with. The little ones did my head in and I was shattered by the end of the day. This was a useful exercise though because it confirmed that the secondary age range was right for me; and I could concentrate on my subject specialism without having to worry about so many other subject areas as well. I certainly recommend people going into school to shadow teachers; it was a real revelation for me. I don't remember being as naughty at school as some of the kids I saw. Something else that surprised me was the style of teaching I saw. When I was at school I hated our PE lessons, as I wasn't very good. I hated having to go out in the freezing cold and do sports I was useless at, with the teacher just reinforcing how useless I was! Our regimental PE teacher was no fun at all. But the PE I saw was really different and innovative. The kids were involved in the lesson, coaching each other and evaluating each other's work. Even those that were not that good seemed to enjoy getting stuck in. I wish it had been like that when I was at school.'

An English student found himself being sold on the idea of becoming a teacher after completing a period of school-based observation. His decision for training to teach English was due to inspiring English lessons at school and university, but it was confirmed once he had made the effort to return to secondary school to complete some voluntary observations:

'I had found A-level English and my university experience quite inspiring, but I was also aware that I had very little recollection of my high school days. School was something that happened in the background while listening to rock music and mumbling sullenly. Revisiting the school environment confirmed for me that this was where I wanted to be, on the other side of the fence, so to speak.'

A History student also supports the idea of spending time in school prior to applying:

'I originally applied for a primary course as the end of my

university course approached and was put on a waiting list. However, I quickly changed my mind and applied for a secondary PGCE after spending time in a primary school and not liking it.'

Gaining an insight into the job cannot be recommended enough. After all, this is the best way to make an informed choice concerning a career move, especially when you may not have a realistic idea of what it entails apart from memories from your own school days.

The influence of your own teachers

It is not only immediate family that seems to be so influential in drawing people towards the profession. It is well documented that teachers are strong role models for youngsters, and carry a great deal of power in their actions. Time and time again reflections from current students reinforce the overriding factor drawing them into the profession as being the lasting impression or influence of one of their own teachers, expressed in comments such as 'there were a couple of teachers who I respected and admired at high school'. An English student remarked:

'I do remember having an inspiring primary school teacher as well as A-level and university lecturers. I felt I could emulate their passion for English, and more importantly, I wanted to try to instil the same passion in others. Although I must also admit that another huge reason for becoming a teacher was because I was not drawn (vehemently opposed more like) to the corporate jobs available!'

'I want to be the next Mr Massey' leapt out from the personal statement on an application form for the secondary Physical Education course. The first question at interview had to be 'Who is Mr Massey?' It transpired that Mr Massey was in fact a teacher from the applicant's own school days:

'He was very influential and liked by all. Everyone held Mr Massey in high esteem and I thought that's what I would like, and choosing to be a PE teacher would enable me to fill his boots, even though it would be like trying to fill a size 9 with a size 6.'

If Mr Massey were to read this, then he would no doubt feel very flattered, as anyone would, knowing they had been so influential in creating such a positive attitude towards a subject. It does appear to be a frequent occurrence for prospective teachers to consider individual teachers when reflecting on influences on their chosen career route, even to identify them precisely in application statements:

> 'Mr Livingstone, he was the person who first got me into sport and the idea of being a teacher, as he was my middle school teacher. He took us outside every day for 45 minutes, doing health-related fitness and athletics so we would always have something every morning. Everyone else would get one PE afternoon a week, but he would say no, I want it every day. He was a fitness fanatic himself and looking at him with his bulging muscles, you would think, yes he is a great role model, and a lot of my friends in my class have gone on to do things in fitness because it was pushed early on.'

The overriding commonality with such references seems to be the love of the subject, which has grown from the example of these powerful role models. How often do youngsters when talking about school relay their enjoyment of a particular subject, not by the content alone but by describing the person presenting that subject? Once again we can see the power we hold in influencing youngsters both in their immediate and longer-term perceptions of the subjects they engage in week after week throughout their school lives.

We must not forget that the power we have to influence may not always be for the better. A PE student described how he was influenced most by two people for different reasons:

> 'My form tutor at school was a big influence. She was a good drama teacher, but I admired her most for the way she dealt with her form group. She was caring, enthusiastic, organised and all the kids respected her. I wanted to have this respect. Unfortunately, I didn't have an ideal role model as a PE teacher, in fact I didn't think they were very good at the job and I thought I could do better. So, I'm trying to be a better role model for my pupils.'

The influence of friends

It's not just family and teachers that may have a lot to answer for in guiding us in our career choice, and in providing a lasting impression. Some students have indicated clearly how friends can help in the decision-making process:

> 'It's mainly the example of my friend who gave me the idea ... and it was fitting with the charity work I wanted to do. For many days, I had no idea on what to do, and in one hour, when the wife of my friend told me how he became a teacher, I had decided to do the same.'

Likewise, a Geography student was also motivated to train to teach by friends who were already teachers, and the intriguing stories they had to tell. In fact, his old boss had already taken the decision to apply and as they chatted and moaned about their current place of work, it suddenly seemed like a good idea for him too: he felt he would be doing something worthwhile rather than lining the pockets of company shareholders!

A calling?

It may be said by some that a career in teaching is a vocation, rather than a job. The following narratives from students seem to support such a notion:

> 'I had always wanted to teach and did my math's degree with the intention of doing a PGCE straight afterwards.'

> 'I always wanted to be a teacher, however, while at college I didn't think I would get the grades to go to university so I didn't apply. However, when my results came they were better than I thought, so here I am.'

> 'Everyone suggested from day one that I should be a teacher because whilst working on an outdoor pursuits camp I tended to have a good affinity with kids, and so I started to look at courses. For me it's about getting into a profession kind of thing and this is something I want to do. My friend has got a £360,000 mortgage and drives a convertible Z3 and he's my age and I sit back and think, yes, you sit in front of a computer

all day and deal with money, that's not me. I am more happy being outside working with kids, teaching the subject I love and being happy with my Renault 5 Campus and my suntan!'

For some individuals the process of choosing teaching as a career appears to be due more to circumstance, as the following examples demonstrate:

'Have idea whilst lying on a beach in Malaysia ...
... dismiss idea, concentrate on relaxing ...
... return home late August ...
... break-up of long-term relationship ...
... drunken conversation with old friend – both resolve to become teachers ...
... apply next morning ...
... get late interview for place on course ...
... move to Norwich and frantically look for a flat!'

'People were applying for jobs whilst at university and I joined the rat race to be employed by a corporate company as a management consultant or HR consultant. I applied for two jobs, had one interview which was horrific and then realised it wasn't my world. I applied late onto the PGCE and the course was sadly full. In fact that was a good thing as I got a basic office administrator's job for a year, which confirmed even more strongly what a bad plan it was to consider these types of jobs. I applied again and haven't looked back. The decision had been there for some time as I nearly applied for an Education Degree but decided it was too restricting, so just did a Biology Degree instead. Having put it off due to the advice I received from current, training and ex-teachers I finally managed to start training.'

'I was doing quite a lot of sports coaching in schools and I really enjoyed helping the children to enjoy sport. It was the little things that used to give me a buzz ... Like watching little Billy (who hadn't been able to hit a ball for two weeks) edge a run to win a game of cricket! It was the feeling of knowing that you had taught the kids how to do something, and that you had also managed to make that child feel good about themselves.'

'It was really itchy feet and the feeling that I was missing out on

something by not working in education. Having grown up with it and with friends in the profession I could see the satisfaction and rewards to be gained from it and realised I wanted to experience those too.'

'*I had been thinking about it on and off for about three years or so. I think I'd even got as far as requesting an application one year, but never got any further. One summer I decided on the spur of the moment to apply, otherwise I'd never know if it was for me. Unfortunately, all the places were full for the following year, but I applied at the earliest opportunity the following year and secured a place.'*

A student who had been a well-paid administrative assistant in the City concurred:

'*Well it sounds really corny now, but I worked in the City and I was getting quite good money, and I was fed up of stepping over homeless people, and of the commercial world. I just felt I had outlived my use for it. And so I wanted to retrain to do something that I thought was really serving the community.'*

And, in the words of another career-changer, who had decided to become a Science teacher:

'*When I gave up my previous position, I wanted to do some charity work, going to India with the Sisters of Charity. The 9/11 tragedy in the United States has changed it all. Many NGOs are importing occidental culture in countries that don't want it; the 9/11 helped me to realise this. So I decided to do my charity work at home (as Mother Theresa said): Physics teachers are missing ... nobody wants to become a teacher, so I decided to do this.'*

Sometimes when realising your vocation, it may not be so easy to realise which age range one is best suited to working with:

'*I began a primary teaching course after leaving school, so teaching was always on my mind. However, I decided to wait until I was a bit older and had some life experience to begin secondary teaching.'*

It is no secret that there is currently a shortage of teachers in certain subjects, with particular difficulty found in recruiting graduates in subjects which command high prices in the industrial marketplace. When one can get a big salary working in business, finance or computing, then the question that begs to be asked is: What is the attraction for anyone to consider taking on the challenge of teaching unruly teenagers? The government has attempted to address this through various lucrative new recruitment incentives, such as training salaries, 'golden hellos' and paying off student loans. One has to wonder as to how long it will be before we see the metaphorical carrot of company cars and holiday vouchers.

Recent recruitment advertising from the Training and Development Agency included captions and slogans such as 'for the indispensable more of the disposable' in relation to paying off student loans for newly qualified teachers in Mathematics, Science subjects, Modern Foreign Languages, English (including Drama), Welsh, Design and Technology and ICT. One of the issues relating to the lack of graduates considering the profession surrounds the financial implications of embarking on further training after three years of university life, or for some, the realities of retraining to make a move from long-established but perhaps unsatisfactory employment:

> 'Having considered teaching after my degree, unfortunately finances did not permit. The advertisements inspired me to make the career move as the funding made it a realistic option.'

Likewise, for this Mathematics student:

> 'I have been toying with the idea for years, but it was before the initiative came in so I couldn't afford the year out. The most important thing was discussing it with my wife and whether she thought I would be a good teacher, having been in school, having seen other teachers. Or did she think I would be somebody that would ooze that negative impression of teaching, because that's my biggest concern, that I'm going to fall into that pit and reinforce that stereotype of "if you can't do, you teach", which they are still trying to shift as you can see by the advertising. I think it's incredibly unfair because the best teachers are certainly people that could do anything they wanted to.'

Many more personal accounts from students have reinforced the fact that the current initiatives have undoubtedly helped the decision-making process to apply, as remarked upon by a Science graduate:

> '*I had lived overseas for a couple of years and was looking for a fresh start, and would have been unable to afford to pay fees or support myself without the training bursary.*'

Each year courses are comprised of a healthy mix of young graduates, fresh from their degrees and university lifestyles, and those who may have taken detours along the way – either by opting out of the rat-race and travelling the globe, starting a family, or leaving an established job or career.

Changing to teaching

Recent research (Priyadharshini and Robinson-Pant, 2003) focused on career changers moving into teaching. It highlighted the very positive fact that some of the new entrants consciously chose teaching in preference to a career in which they were already established. There was a strong consensus that having 'life experience' is certainly something that many entrants to the profession value. The research identified six different profiles for career changers: the parent, the successful careerist, the freelancer, the late starter, the serial careerist, and the young career changer. Many respondents, particularly women, identified being a 'parent' as their most recent experience prior to joining the course. Careers prior to starting a family had included medical research, television reporting, law and the RAF. Coupled with the decision to return to the workforce, there was the belief that teaching had a more 'family friendly' image as compared to their previous careers or other potential careers.

All students bring to the process of learning to teach a wealth of previous experience, none more so than 'the successful careerist', identified by the research as the first type of career changer. Successful careerists are mostly professionals, who have done well in industry or business, having followed a particular career since university where they had acquired the necessary qualifications and training. Examples of the careers that people in this category had moved from included law, editing, management, accounting, insurance, engineering, information technology, and teaching English as a foreign language. One interesting issue to emerge from the interviews with these career changers revealed a common realisation that they were taking a risk in moving from an established career at a later stage in their lives, entailing not just a considerable drop in salary, but also, initially, a drop in status by becoming a student. The second category of career changer identified was that of serial careerists, individuals who had moved frequently from career to career, having several short, successful and often well-paid careers.

A student for English teaching previously worked as a Civil Servant, taking on the extra challenge of an Open University Degree at the same time. It was during the period of studying that she seriously considered continuing her studying with a teacher preparation course. Unfortunately, once the degree finished, she was no longer in a position to do so. Life went on, and a few years later, having left the Civil Service with a Masters Degree under her belt, she decided the time was right to start learning to teach.

The financial implications of embarking on re-training can be a major factor for some applicants considering a major change of direction in their careers. A Mathematics student, who had decided to leave the world of the Tax Office to re-train, highlighted this:

> 'The change around in the government's strategy to fund initial teacher training means it's not as a big a gamble and it's not now something that is going to completely break the bank. There was no other way I could have funded it, without the £6000.'

Some people who were dissatisfied with the rationale underpinning their previous jobs stated this as a major reason for their career change, as a former medical researcher emphasised:

> 'In an office it is about you, you, you. But in teaching ... it's not so selfish. I want a job where I can have an effect. The idea that they are actively looking for teachers made a difference to me. I thought they really want me; it is a chalk-face job making a difference, whereas research never had that. I felt as a teacher you have a real impact, being part of the community.'

The third category of career changer identified by the research was the freelancer. These people had followed a single career, but were often employed on short-term contracts. Examples include

artistic decorators, translators, actors and 'English as a foreign language' teachers.

The late starter was the fourth category of career changer, which included those who had left school with few or no qualifications and had gone straight into the job market, choosing to enter higher education at a later age than the most frequently selected time. In contrast to this, there was also the young career changer, mostly graduates who had left university with debts to pay off, opting for a lucrative first job. A few years on, they were looking for more fulfilling careers.

The research highlighted the sheer magnitude of life experience being brought into the profession and the sheer variety of backgrounds and contexts that future teachers come from.

For some, it just takes a little longer to identify one's vocation:

> *'I have always held teachers in high respect, and although I thought my personality would suit teaching, I did not have enough to offer as a 21-year-old graduate. I spent five years travelling through developing and Westernised countries, to see what was around, before I decided what I wanted. This made me appreciate my background more and realise how important education is. I tried many lines of work. In looking for a satisfying, varied, worthwhile job that included the option of travelling internationally, I arrived at teaching again. Not wanting to wait another year, I travelled almost immediately back to England and had applied to four institutions in areas I would like to live, within a fortnight.'*

Applications for training

As far as the recruiting provider is concerned, the applicants' Graduate Teacher Training Recruitment form is the starting point in the selection process, summarising the nature of the first degree held and previous experience that may support the application, particularly in relation to working with youngsters. The process also involves getting to know a little about the applicant through their personal statement. Of course, the interview itself should be a two-way process, with the applicant making an informed choice as to their chosen route for learning to teach:

> *'The interviewer talked me more into it, because when I was in*

the interview I brought in a folder of work I had done. There was work I had done that I did not even realise would benefit me. When I explained how I was doing my job I hadn't seen the connection of being a team leader and looking after a team of instructors, I hadn't seen the connection with the whole tutor role, so my listening skills have come through as an important strength to my application.'

And as far as a Mathematics student is concerned, he made an informed choice to pursue the PGCE route, identifying the features he found to be right for him:

'I looked at the various routes for training. My wife persuaded me because she had been through a PGCE so I had her experiences to draw from ... Although everybody on the PGCE course has been in teaching, they are now dedicated to the education of teachers ... I think it's the best way to enter teaching, when you are surrounded by lots different ideas, lots of different people throwing in their tuppence-worth and saying "I did it like this", you are playing off each other to get ideas.'

Such sentiment is endorsed by Capel, Leask and Turner (1999), highlighting the fact that induction into a profession takes time: 'It is best conducted within institutional partnerships that offer strong personal support, ample resources and generous opportunities to work in real school settings.'

Sharing these many personal and varied narratives has possibly shed some light into some of the motives for wanting to learn about learning and the aspiration of becoming a teacher. Such insights may also strike a chord with the motives that practising teachers have with regard to their own reasons for choosing teaching as a career path. One could say that it's in the blood, particularly with so many students indicating the family trait of being part of the teaching fraternity. The influence of existing teachers within one's own family, or that of friends or teachers from one's own school days, is certainly a strong factor, along with a genuine passion for a particular subject. These are all variables identified by current students as to why they have chosen to opt into teaching. However, the message that also appears to come through is that the decision-making process is

complicated for many. This has been clearly documented by the research on the many career changes that embark on the new career journey.

One director of a teacher preparation course always welcomes new students with an introductory talk, stating that the best thing course tutors could do would be to inject all students with ten years' worth of experience, if only that were possible. This has had an impact on a Geography student, who said:

> 'Teaching is predominantly having a bank of experiences that you can draw upon so that you can say to yourself I know how to teach this topic, I know how to deal with this situation, I know how to get the best out of this class, then constantly refining all that. I think that's really what this course is trying to do, to bring people up to speed as quickly as possible by getting other people's experience and hopefully a bit will rub off and then you can put your own slant on it.'

So, the reality of learning to teach can be best summarised by the words of a PE student:

> 'The reality was quite daunting, I didn't expect to be dreaming about lesson plans and how lessons are going to go. Waking up in the middle of the night saying that will be an excellent drill, writing it down on a bit of paper and then going back to sleep a happier man.'

But don't let the thought of sleepless nights prevent you from joining the profession. The following comments from a student sum up her experience and hopefully demonstrate the exciting time ahead:

> 'Having had the idea that I would enjoy and be good at teaching for a long time, I was rather anxious about what the reality would be like, especially with little experience of children. My relief at absolutely loving being a teacher keeps putting a smile on my face. Enjoying and being quite good at communicating with the children is a great relief. Revising and learning in my subject is filling me with more enthusiasm than I had when completing my degree. The university component has been a very interesting learning curve in places. Very few days, I

thought, were a waste, and I can't think of how I could have been prepared any better than I am for being in the classroom. The PGCE is just an initiation to see whether teaching is for you and whether you are for it.'

Chapter 2

Learning about teaching

Jeff Battersby

Training to become a teacher is often a roller-coaster of positive and less than positive experiences. There are so many and varied demands throughout the period of training, but especially when on school placement. Planning the learning experiences of numerous pupils and classes, standing in front of a class for the first time, dealing with less than enthusiastic pupils, making sense of the plethora of advice being offered, marking and assessing umpteen essays, artefacts and newspaper articles all by tomorrow is what makes the year such a memorable one. This chapter celebrates the most positive experiences, helpful advice and those special moments which enabled the student teachers to rise and meet their greatest challenges as they learned about teaching.

The challenges of learning to teach

> '*Motivating myself to get up early, drive for an hour, sit through meetings, teach for five hours a day dealing with fires, fights, friends, graffiti, failing bloomin' QTS skills tests, coming home planning and marking 'til midnight. Apart from that I have loved every moment!*'

This observation captures the whole experience of learning to teach and some of the richness and reality of the training year. So what is it that drives and motivates people to come into teaching and to undergo a really intensive period of training, such as the year completing the PGCE? What are the significant moments for them, the highs and the lows, the achievements and the times when things appear to go 'pear-shaped'? At what point do student teachers grit their teeth and make a real go of it or choose to throw in the towel? At what moment do they see a future for themselves as teachers? How do they know that they are being successful and developing as newly emerging teachers? How do they learn about teaching?

Answers to some of these questions emerge from an identification of the challenges faced during training by student teachers themselves, from their experiences gained in classrooms, from the plethora of advice offered to them from mentors, tutors, peers, textbooks and learned journals which espouse theoretical insights into teaching, learning, assessment and classroom management. Even the pupils themselves will offer advice and comment, whether called for or not!

> 'One of the quiet, well-behaved girls in my "nightmare year 9 class" said "How come you never tell anyone off?" This made me realise this class had become a nightmare because I was letting it.'

> 'A year 8 pupil told me I needed more activities in the lesson rather than just giving information.'

Learning the hard way

During an observation of one of my student teachers teaching a mixed-ability year 8 class, it soon became clear that the lesson was not going according to plan, in fact it was disintegrating before our eyes. Whilst some careful planning had occurred for this lesson as an individual lesson, the student teacher had not considered how little the group had achieved in the previous lesson and that they were engrossed in the tasks that had been set for that last lesson. The student teacher manfully, or in this case womanfully, tried to instil some discipline into the class and tried to engage them in the new learning planned for this lesson, despite their protestations that they needed to complete their last task, which involved the pupils working in groups. The frustration mounted for all in the class, the student teacher wishing to put on a 'good performance' in front of her tutor and the class wanting to complete a piece of work for which they were clearly motivated. Annoyance and resentment were building between the student teacher and her class, as well as the class with the student teacher.

The lesson was becoming a battle-ground, with names put on the whiteboard, threats of detentions and pupils being sent to their year head coming from the student teacher. Shouts of 'It's not fair' were coming from the pupils, coupled with lots of questions relating to the previous lesson's tasks to be completed. There had been an implicit assumption on their part, perhaps suggested by the student teacher, that time would be given to complete the task started last lesson. The pupils were operating as a group intent on manipulating the situation to what they perceived had been agreed last lesson. The student teacher realised that the lesson she had planned for today was never going to take place and so she abandoned it, deciding that it would indeed be better to continue with the tasks from the previous lesson than start something new. Once this decision had been made and conveyed, the class were transformed and there was a buzz about the classroom as the pupils became actively engaged in their work.

The student teacher recovered her lesson, her relationship with the pupils became more positive, there was a good working atmosphere in the classroom and the pupils were purposefully engaged in learning. Unfortunately the student teacher could not identify with this positive development. She was sure that she had failed. At the end of the lesson, once all the pupils had departed in an orderly way, she burst into tears stating that the lesson had been an absolute failure and that she was giving up teaching this minute. I assured her that this perceived failure was far from the case and that she had demonstrated a great recovery, taking the lesson from a potentially failing one to one where there was much successful learning occurring and one which was well managed. Had she continued with her planned lesson and not been able to instil her authority on the class, then she would most probably have demonstrated a failing lesson.

It is in situations such as these that we can learn so much about our own teaching, about pupil learning and about classroom management. The discussions following the 'disastrous' lesson were full and frank, emotional and wearing, yet constructive and positive. There was a successful outcome to this situation, to the school placement, and now the student teacher is enjoying success as a new teacher.

So how typical was this event and how do student teachers learn about teaching? Throughout each school placement student teachers are constantly reflecting and evaluating their performance and specifically how effective their lessons were in terms of meeting a range of teaching and learning objectives. Frequent observation of student teachers' teaching by mentors and tutors feed into this evaluation of performance, providing evidence of capability in relation to the QtT Standards. At the end of each placement there is also an opportunity to stand back and take stock, to reflect on the whole experience in order to identify specific strengths and areas for further development for these newly emerging teachers.

The greatest challenges

One of the most significant challenges is the change from learner to teacher yet being both at the same time, learning and developing pedagogy simultaneously. Coming to terms with the subject matter to be taught, the need to identify and to cater for a wide range of abilities, of different preferred learning styles, choosing which strategy to adopt from a wide range of teaching and learning strategies to suit particular pupils and classes, pitching the content of the lesson appropriately and all of this in ever-changing circumstances, time of day, week, year, pupil dynamics, classroom environment and the charisma of the teacher you are taking over from.

The weather seems to transform classes too: thunder and lightening, snow storms, windy days all appear to excite pupils, hot and humid days make them lethargic and tetchy. Lessons before and after lunch are problematic either because the blood-sugar levels have dropped too low or the exertions of the playground have left them exhausted and too tired to concentrate. As for the last lesson on Friday afternoon . . . .

Getting started is hard enough

Standing in front of a class for the first time was one of the biggest challenges identified by almost all student teachers:

> 'Getting up and staying up to take my first lesson ... there are so many things that you've to remember ... it was difficult enough to not trip over the OHP lead, let alone remember which way to move it to make the writing bigger. From there it got so much better.'

'To overcome my fear of talking to large groups and not get my words muddled up, all you want to do is hide in a corner!'

'Gaining the same respect from pupils as a "proper teacher". It can be quite demoralising to have a rowdy group quieten down as soon as a "real teacher" comes in.'

This becomes an even bigger challenge when you 'take over classes who are happy with their "normal" teacher and resent change', especially when this might be at a crucial time in their work programmes and any assessment period including mock exams, SATS, or GCSE coursework. On the other hand, you might be the breath of fresh air that the class needs to engage and invigorate them into learning.

'Teaching the very first lesson was nerve-racking, but that was a good experience as well because I never felt that nervous again!'

And now:

'. . . realising at the end of the course how easy it is!'

Workload and time management

Coming to terms with the workload, especially when on school placement, was the most significant challenge for many student teachers:

'Learning to cope with everything you have to deal with: planning, management, assessment, admin., all demand your attention and feeling overwhelmed can happen at anytime in the course. It is very easy to be disheartened and sometimes other people/colleagues will be able to pick up on this. The most important thing I have learned is not to try to cope on your own when it gets too much but SPEAK OUT – you will get the advice and support you need if you ask for it.'

Inevitably in the early stages of the course and specifically when on placement

> *'planning lessons took hours and I was constantly exhausted'*

which caused some resentment for some student teachers as they tried to come to terms with

> *'combating tiredness and … coping with the lack of free time and not having a life … finding time for socialising and knowing when to stop! You always feel as if you could do loads more worksheets for a lesson, but you can only do so much and must put it away and say that'll do.'*

> *'I cannot stress enough how important time management and organising myself is and how much it can impact on your life if you aren't.'*

> *'What is needed is a crash course into being a "professional" – how to separate (and where to draw the line) work and personal life … finding time for myself and not feeling guilty about it.'*

Once into the swing of lesson planning and surviving whole lessons with groups of pupils, then time management of pupils' learning within lessons and over the course of a unit of teaching posed other significant challenges:

> *'Being able to visualise a lesson, predicting the amount of time that should be spent on an activity … There is not enough time to do everything and so establishing priorities is essential … It is necessary to stop one task when allotted time has run out and go on to the next task, otherwise you fall behind and start to panic, and once this occurs you begin to work inefficiently and ineffectively and lose more time.'*

(Notwithstanding my earlier observations of the student teacher and her year 8 class!)

Whilst there is a need to 'plan well, do not be overly concerned if you do not get through all the work you set out to do. Progress at a rate suitable to the pupils in each particular group' was offered from another student. You can always 'Try something different next time; after all, this is teaching practice.'

Knowing your subject

'Learn how to spin a yarn and tell a good story and they will generally shut up and listen.'

This advice was given to a number of student teachers as they were preparing to go into their first teaching placement. Having a wealth of stories and anecdotes to draw on is enormously helpful to offer illustration and exemplification to your teaching, but be wary of falling into the trap of being the 'class bore', the 'I've been everywhere, done it and got the T-shirt man', and forget the holiday snaps.

Acquiring sufficient or appropriate subject knowledge to teach concerned many student teachers. Those who had completed their degree some time ago, or where the degree itself bore limited reference to the subject taught in school, created a significant challenge to some who identified difficulties boosting and updating their subject knowledge ... 're-learning my A-level subject' ... to be ... 'competent in my subject' ... as well as the challenge posed in bringing the intellectual level of the subject within the understanding of a low-ability group. 'Judging what different age groups will have as background knowledge'; 'it's easy to under- or over-estimate what different age groups will know'. This issue of competent subject knowledge is explored in greater depth in the following chapter.

For some their greatest challenge was trying to 'understand netball!' either as a PE student or a non-specialist who is teaching games as an extra strand to their practice. Almost all trainees were able to identify some aspect of their own subject that they had some difficulty with or areas of the subject that they had never encountered in their own learning. Having a secure knowledge and understanding of your specialist subject is of crucial importance because 'if you're not sure what you are really doing, this affects the pupils attitude and behaviour'. It is better to admit your lack of knowledge and suggest to the pupils that they might like to find the answer for next lesson rather than providing a public demonstration of your failings as an expert in your subject or wrestling with uncertainty over your response. So bluffing and blagging are out!

Classroom management – sorted!

Achieving effective classroom control was the most significant challenge for many student teachers 'trying to maintain classroom control with my low-ability year 9 class!' This was particularly true in the early stages of teaching when

> *'a lot of the class didn't think of me as a "proper teacher" and were reluctant to listen to my instructions and do any work ... I began by giving lots of detentions ... then I found that by using positive strategies (for example, one house point for anyone getting to Question 3) the class responded.'*

Clearly behaviourist theory in practice!
  Equally,

> *'... knowing how to react in certain situations, what is most effective ... dealing with pupils who won't take responsibility for learning ...'*

Classroom management continues to be a concern for most student teachers throughout the year on each school placement and with many of their classes. This is not unusual and remains a concern probably for most teachers, even those with considerable experience. There are always some pupils who fail to be switched on to learning, however dynamic and exciting the lesson presented to them is. The message given to most student teachers on any course is 'don't smile before Christmas'. Appearing to be the pupils' friend, being easy-going and pleasant to them right from the first encounter might win them over initially, but in practice everything is more likely to end in tears. Some student teachers learnt from their experiences of smiling too soon, too easily, generally being too soft, inconsistent and failing to pick up on the small indiscretions:

> *'Try not to be the pupils' friend ... as when I started I was eager for the pupils to like me. But, as I progressed, I realised that we are there to be teachers and not there to be friends. Once I realised this I felt more confident in myself, and the pupils, I feel, had more respect for me ... Make sure that the ground rules are established before you begin building a friendly atmosphere in the classroom.'*

'I did not "go in hard" at the start and after an initial week's honeymoon with the kids behaving well, they suddenly turned ... working to re-establish myself with this class was my biggest challenge.'

And from another student teacher who had had some experience of teaching English as a second language to pupils who

'... actually wanted to be there and learn ... I stated sanctions but failed to follow them through, consequently my authority was undermined. However, as soon as I started carrying out my sanctions, I found the pupils behaved better and had more respect for me.'

Sometimes the classroom management problems occur because of

'lack of pens, books, textbooks, pupils arriving late, having to leave early, sickness, truancy, Successmaker [widely used educational software], messing around, being off task ... so sometimes I felt I was running out of strategies.'

So the best advice from one of the student teachers is to 'start as you mean to go on and don't waver. I didn't, and had to work twice as hard.'

At different points of the course and certainly during school placement, particular events or moments can have a very telling impact on your teaching. The following examples illustrate the determination of the student teachers to tackle the problems they were facing and adopt strategies to deal with them. They were not going to give up easily or be beaten:

'I really raised my voice for the first time with my chatty and noisy year 8 group to say "this noise level is unacceptable!" The class were all a bit shocked that I had shouted and went silent immediately! From then on I realised that by shouting occasionally (or even lowering my voice a bit) the class went quiet.'

It is important to impose yourself on the class that you are teaching to create and manage a positive working environment in your classroom to enable pupils to engage in learning. Often, pupils are unaware of the noise level and need to be given either a gentle, or in some cases a firm reminder to reduce the noise level. It is not a requirement that all pupils should be quiet at all times in all lessons for you to meet the QtT Standards. There will be times when you really want the pupils to raise their voices, be excited and engaged in a passionate debate over a particularly sensitive or controversial issue, as long as everything is under your control and planned for!

Most schools have behaviour policies which detail procedures and action to be taken in specific circumstances where pupils misbehave. It is important that you get to know these policies as quickly as possible and take appropriate action so that the pupils know that they are expected to behave for you as they would for all other teachers in the school. When you are on placement you have the 'authority' of the teacher, but equally the responsibility that goes with this and the need to act as all other teachers do within the school to 'enforce' the policies. Presenting a united front to the pupils, providing a consistency of approach and reaction to any transgressions or deviation from the expected, enables everyone to know where they stand and the likely consequences if they do not adhere to the 'rules'.

The following reflections illustrate how important it is to develop your classroom management skills, to have a range of effective strategies at your disposal and the confidence to adopt these in appropriate circumstances:

> 'I had an awful period 5 Friday lesson with a year 10 class which pushed me to the limit as their behaviour was appalling and really got to me. From this point on I recognised in a new way the importance of maintaining the classroom behaviour plan. Having seen things go wrong really encouraged me to be firmer and not let anything go. So, though it was a terrible experience it did improve my classroom management skills.'

> 'My year 9 class had been really good whilst I was being observed, but as soon as my mentor left me unsupervised the class became really difficult. This made me realise that my strategies for classroom management needed to be changed and once I had done so the pupils became much more responsive.'

> 'I was faced with a challenging year 7 class and throughout the lesson I remained calm (and just about in control). I proved

that I was capable of dealing with classes by myself and my confidence grew. From this experience I learnt to evaluate and deal with situations as they arose.'

'With one particular difficult group I really lost my temper with them, but then regained my composure and spoke to them about how they were messing up chances for others and it's not fair. After this they seemed to see why they should behave.'

'The first time that I sent one boy who was disrupting the lesson to the isolation room changed the way I dealt with behaviour, showing the class who was in charge.'

'I kept my cool, moved a few of them, sent a couple out, kept very calm and strangely I actually enjoyed the experience of being able to deal with the problems.'

'Laying down my expectations for behaviour early on. I explained what I expected and they had to stick to these rules.'

All of this with very pleasing consequences: 'Cracking the behaviour problem made the group a pleasure to teach and easier to experiment with.'

Planning for learning

'Having a whole day's teaching and being unprepared for one lesson was disastrous. It made me rethink my planning strategy to redevelop my lesson plan sheet and prepare all my lessons a week in advance.'

The question that never goes away for as long as you teach is 'What am I going to do with them next lesson?' In most cases you will have some reasonably clear idea because you will be able to refer to the school's or department's scheme of work for the particular class you are taking. There will be a clear indication of the aims and learning objectives for the unit of work with a statement of the intended learning outcomes, suggestions for activities and tasks, resources to use together with the timing and mode of assessment of the pupils' learning. It is important to adhere to these guidelines as other classes in the same year group will be following the same ones and all classes will be assessed in the same way against them.

Some schools will give you some flexibility in relation to the scheme of work, others will insist on you following them to the letter. Some schools will emphasise the overall learning objectives and outcomes and be less constraining when it comes to specific exemplification and resources. Some will insist on specific texts and case studies to be used. All schemes of work fit into an overall department plan for each of the year groups. It will be inappropriate for you to simply decide for yourself which video extract to use, topic to cover or book to introduce to your class in place of the set text. It is important for you to know what is expected of you before you embark on your teaching and your preparation.

When planning your next lesson, you should be aware of the pupils' prior learning. This will inevitably be rather sketchy when you start on your school placement, particularly when you are new to the school and you are unaware of their previous teaching. However, once you have taught that first lesson you will become increasingly aware of the strengths and needs of individuals within the group as well as the class as a whole. This growing knowledge will be used to inform and refine your planning of their next lesson.

Each lesson should provide opportunities for the pupils to develop their knowledge, understanding and skills in relation to the subject, or contribute to the development of the core skills of literacy, numeracy, ICT, communication, working with others and problem solving. Your lesson plan will identify the specific knowledge that the pupils will acquire and how they will develop their understanding of this new knowledge or concept through specific tasks and activities. Overall, you will need to identify what your pupils are going to be able to do at the end of the lesson that they wouldn't have been able to do at the beginning.

Two pieces of sound advice from experienced inexperienced teachers towards the end of their school placements: you should always 'emphasise the learning rather than the teaching' and 'look at the lesson from the pupils' perspective'.

I am sure that advice was given in the first week, but might not have been internalised at that point. The major emphasis and purpose of each lesson is to create positive learning opportunities for the pupils to enable them to develop and progress their knowledge, understanding and skills. The effectiveness of your 'teaching', which includes the planning, preparation, resourcing and management of the lesson, will be judged against this.

The second piece of advice is so obvious, yet not always adhered to. It is all too easy to think about the knowledge that you want the pupils to acquire that lessons can end up with content overload and be simply information giving. Student teachers can fall into the trap of thinking that because the information has been given to the pupils it is therefore known and understood by them. As you will remember from the time you were learning to drive, had to assemble a pre-packed piece of furniture or tried to give directions to someone new to an area, the connections between knowing what you have to do, understanding how to do it and having the skills to carry it out are not always apparent.

As teachers we appear really good at constructing interesting questions and tasks for pupils to engage with, but we rarely see these from the pupils' perspective or try to complete them ourselves. We become aware of the complexity, ambiguity and shortcomings of our instructions and the impossibility of the task when the pupils hand in their work for assessment. When this occurs, how far will you go and hold up your hands, apologise and take responsibility for this apparent confusion and not penalise the pupils for their inability to read your mind?

At any stage of development as a teacher it is worth heeding these following observations:

> 'A bad lesson with year 8 in which they were very disruptive just made me more determined to improve my plans and made me stricter.'

> 'A horrible first lesson with a year 7 group forced me to re-evaluate my approach and plan for their learning ability.'

> 'I suddenly realised at the end of my second year 9 lesson that I was putting in all the effort and so the pupils were quite passive. I tried to turn the lessons round ensuring that they were more pupil centred. This helped change my role from one as instructor to one of facilitator.'

Planning for learning is of paramount importance and unless you have developed competence in this aspect and are conscientious in it you will struggle to develop as a competent teacher. Having an effective plan for the lesson and for pupils' learning will enable you to teach the lesson with greater confidence and it is more likely that the pupils will engage in the learning you have planned for them. The poor experience identified above led the student teacher to take his mentor's advice and 'plan lessons in advance and never be afraid to ask for help'. This help can come from mentors and other teachers in your placement school or even from your colleagues on the course. Your peers can be a tower of strength to you and provide a wealth of knowledge, ideas and advice for you to capitalise on and should be used to the full.

Another successful strategy adopted by many student teachers is to work closely with experienced teachers in school, so that:

> '*Seeing/observing teachers teach lower-ability groups and planning these lessons with them then, step by step, I began to improve my planning and to understand why my lessons hadn't worked.*'

Whilst we all want to teach memorable lessons and ensure that the pupils will be engaged in worthwhile learning, 'what matters are the beginnings and endings of lessons, this is what the pupils will remember'. This is likely to be the case in the majority of lessons, so you will need to plan the starter and plenary sections of your lesson carefully to ensure that the key learning objectives are identified and realised.

Most of our learning occurs when we wrestle with new ideas and constructs which challenge our existing knowledge, understanding and perceptions. In lessons this is enabled by offering pupils opportunities to engage in a variety of learning activities. These need to be planned, worthwhile, rigorous and be fit for purpose. Care is needed to ensure that all planned tasks and activities meet this objective. Some lessons feature too many different activities which disable rather than enable learning to occur, some are simple time fillers to keep pupils occupied with little purpose or challenge to them.

Observation and evaluation

Throughout the course your teaching will be scrutinised by experienced teachers and tutors who will offer their observations and reflections on the evidence generated by your lesson planning and preparation, your teaching performance, classroom management and the achievements of the pupils set against the planned learning outcomes for them. Some observations will be very specific and relate to particular strategies, incidents, moments and individuals in the lesson. Others will comment on your overall achievements as well as specific targets which you will need to address in order to progress to become a competent practitioner.

You are encouraged, most likely required, to evaluate each of your lessons to enable you to plan for the next one with that same group, or a similar one. At the end of each lesson it is all too easy to find fault with your personal performance, the noise level within the class, the perceived lack of work completed or the lack of engagement by the pupils. Teachers, and student teachers in particular, rarely identify and celebrate the successes that have been created within the lesson for individual pupils or the class as a whole. The perfect lesson has yet to be taught, so for most of us the failings in the lesson, the things that went wrong or the individuals, incidents and interruptions that caused problems are the most noteworthy. It is important to present an honest evaluation of all aspects of teaching and learning following each lesson and unit of work. This enables us to reflect on our personal performance as well as that of the pupils, the scale, scope and challenge of the work set and lessons to be learnt for the future when we next teach that particular group or topic.

> 'Having a lesson where pupils have been really well-motivated or contributed lots of ideas ... seeing a group of pupils really interested and involved in an activity I had planned ... being totally blown away by the quality of work I got from the whole group.'

Each of these snippets, from evaluations of their teaching, enabled the student teachers to analyse critically and objectively, their planning, the range of strategies adopted as well as the nature, challenge and management of the topic and the tasks presented to the pupils. The more thorough the evaluation, the more useful it is for future planning and the development of personal competence as a teacher. Some strategies, resources and activities which have been introduced and tried for the first time should be evaluated, especially if they have been identified as specific targets for you to address or where you have identified them as appropriate for this class or for individual pupils within the class.

> '... using activities which involve classroom talk, group work,

games and competitions. When I was at school we never did any activities like this, it was always "chalk and talk". It is very positive to see that these interactive activities can and do work ...'

'Using a piece of literature and a mind movie to help pupils empathise with a topic. Pupils become totally absorbed in the topic and feedback was excellent. Group work in general, whilst taking a lot of effort to set up, always ensured an enjoyable class with a high level of contribution.'

'The experience of trying different methods to calm the class to aid my teaching was invaluable.'

These positive observations by the student teachers themselves enabled them to make decisions for their future planning, to continue with the strategies and approaches they had tried out successfully with their classes or to extend the range of these in future lessons.

Learning from feedback

Learning about their own teaching and how they have enabled pupils to learn and to achieve is drawn from numerous positive experiences that student teachers have had on their school placements. Many cite references to written and verbal observations made by tutors, mentors, pupils and parents. References too to those occasions when they have been valued and appreciated by their pupils and their colleagues in school, where those 'difficult pupils' have come good in their end of unit tests, lessons which went like a dream with all pupils purposefully engaged in worthwhile tasks which challenged and motivated them are particular highlights and proud moments including 'seeing your lesson repeated by another member of staff'.

The mutual sense of achievement for student teachers and their pupils is summed up by the following observations:

'The look on pupils' faces when they have understood something, enjoyed something or said thank you ... the moment when the penny drops ... and marking the end of unit tests, it is lovely to see how well the pupils have done and realise that it is because I have taught them it!'

'When the pupils have made nice comments on how well they understand me and that I'm a good teacher.'

'A year 11 pupil stopped me in the corridor after her last exam and thanked me for all the help I had given her. This makes it all worthwhile.'

This coupled with an observation from a mentor, 'you've done a lot more with that group than you think'.

Advice from all quarters

Student teachers are given a great deal of advice from tutors, mentors and other teachers in schools, from research literature and books offering 101 useful tips in order to build their confidence, set them targets and enable them to be successful practitioners. Equally, by the end of their year they are able to offer advice to their peers and to those who follow them into training. Some emphasise that you should not take everything personally, especially about your performance as a teacher or from the poor behaviour, attitude or (limited) work output of the pupils:

'Remain calm, avoid shouting and confrontation with pupils in the classroom ... Don't take things personally, especially comments from pupils about your lesson ... Don't take bad behaviour personally. This really helped me keep calm when the pupils were playing up ... Don't feel that pupils are having a go at you because you are the teacher, they might have problems at home or could be having a bad day.'

'Everyone has bad lessons, even the best of us' was an observation made by a senior teacher after a bad lesson on a Friday afternoon.

'Listen to other teachers' experiences within the staff room. Share problems with your curriculum group so you realise you are not alone with your problems.'

'Just "roll with the punches".'

Here's some further advice relating to teaching and to lessons:

'*Develop routines structuring the beginning of each lesson.*'

Remember 'the importance of a quick start, it sets the tone for a lesson.'

'*During the course of the lesson ask yourself if the pupils are ready to move on, has the atmosphere changed, have pupils achieved? Then take appropriate action.*'

'*Ask yourself the questions: What is this activity about? And why are you doing it?*'

'*When planning a 60-minute lesson, don't feel you have to cover all of the material; sometimes you only get half or even a quarter covered but that doesn't make you a bad teacher.*'

Though remember the caution earlier and the expectation of your mentor and of the school to cover the planned unit of work. Time lost in some lessons can often be made up in others:

'*Let the pupils know the timings of tasks and keep reminding them how long they have left.*'

'*It's easy to get carried away on one task or activity and forget time. Watching the clock and giving time limits to pupils keeps them on task and develops a pace in the lesson.*'

Ask, don't tell

I have noticed that many student teachers, and even some experienced teachers, tend to talk too much in the classroom. There is a demonstration of the teacher as the fount of subject knowledge, imparting all that is known and relevant to the pupils rather than eliciting this knowledge from the pupils. As has been stated earlier, the role of the teacher is to enable the pupils to demonstrate their knowledge and understanding to you as their teacher as well as to themselves and to their peers. To enable this to happen you need to *ask rather than tell*. Responses to questions will enable you to consider and construct further questions that need to be asked to enable the pupil(s) to progress and achieve.

Pause after you have asked a question to enable the pupils to consider whether they have understood the question, whether they have the appropriate answer to respond, and then either the confidence or disposition to make a public response.

Give out worksheets before explanation. All too often student teachers talk the pupils through tasks or refer to resources which are on a worksheet without giving the worksheet to the pupils beforehand. There is a misguided impression that the pupils will all start on the tasks and not listen to the teacher's instructions or explanation. This can occur and it is important to have the pupils' attention whenever you are talking to them. However, when considering how most of us operate either at home or work with conversations, television and other background noises constantly jostling our concentration, pupils are very adept at switching in when the need arises and switching off when there is no perceived relevance to them. Some pupils will take cognitive holidays from the words of wisdom you are imparting, so it will be for you to decide how far all eyes and ears need to be on you.

Stand back and observe your lesson to admire all that you have created. There are too few opportunities when you are able to reflect on how the lesson you have planned, the strategies you have adopted and the tasks and activities you have set up are working in practice. It is in these moments that you will learn a great deal about your teaching, the clarity of your instructions, the suitability and organisation of the tasks, your classroom management strategies and the capability of your pupils. Taking 'time out' in this way is not a 'cop-out' and you should not feel guilty that you are not haring around the classroom interrogating every child to ascertain their degree of confidence in the work being attempted. Sometimes, probably far too often, we are a constant interruption and irritant to the pupils, asking questions, checking progress ad nauseum. It's no wonder they don't complete anything in the lesson! That being said, it is important that we monitor pupils' progress during the lesson, a requirement of the QtT Standards.

And another thing

Don't reinvent the wheel. It is appropriate to use resources and worksheets already in existence, though it is also important that you do create some yourself and leave in the school when you complete your placement so that you make a contribution to the wealth of resources in the school.

> *Do your marking at school, and when marking the tests do all question one first and then all question two.*
>
> *Make use of non-teaching time in school to free up evenings and weekends.*
>
> *Be yourself.*
>
> *Maintain a sense of humour.*
>
> *And always remember that 3:30 comes no matter what!*

In it together

The whole training experience, particularly being involved with fellow student teachers, created many positive moments and relationships:

> 'The sense of camaraderie which developed. I can almost liken it to the spirit of an army in war time. This was helpful in two ways: in sharing ideas and resources and in terms of moral support in difficult times.'
>
> 'The sense of closeness within our curriculum group and level of support that this has given ... usually during midnight email sessions.'

So having learnt how student teachers learn about teaching, the clear message is to:

> 'Slow down, pace yourself and take measures to avoid burnout ... It's a long distance not a sprint ...'

So, 'Don't forget to breathe!'

For some student teachers their biggest challenge was not related to their teaching and struggling with a bottom set of year 9 pupils, but using 'apostrophes in my assignments' appropriately and consistently. But that's another story or another chapter.

Chapter 3

Learning about your subject

Nalini Boodhoo

Learning to teach is a developmental process and part of that process involves coming to terms with learning about your subject. But what does 'learning about your subject' mean? This very question was explored with a group of students from a number of secondary subject disciplines. What is written in this chapter has been drawn from an extended conversation with the students after they had responded to a questionnaire. The questionnaire and conversations focussed on unpicking the notion of how students learn about their subject during their teacher preparation year and what that process is like. Issues discussed encompassed areas such as whether the students felt sufficiently secure to teach their specialist and second subjects given their own prior learning, how they came to terms with learning about the requirements of their subject in relation to the 11–19 curriculum, and their strategies for improving subject knowledge during the course. So what is the road to learning about one's subject like? What are the concerns that students have when learning to teach their subject? These are the questions that this chapter considers.

The qualifying to teach standards

During teacher preparation courses, learning about the various aspects of one's subject specialism is given a very high priority. Courses are often structured to enable you to gain an understanding of the criteria for the award of Qualified Teacher Status and to achieve them through various combinations of lectures, seminars and school-based experience. Possessing a good understanding of the subjects you will teach, and the ability to deliver lessons which demonstrate that pupils are learning, are central to the frameworks within which Initial Teacher Education operates. Indeed, the Qualifying to Teach standards (TTA, 2003) indicate that teachers are required to:

> ... have a secure knowledge and understanding of the subject(s) ...

and that

> knowledge and understanding should be at a standard equivalent to degree level. (DfES, 2003: 7)

It is also relevant to note that at the heart of these standards is the notion that teachers should be able to *apply* knowledge and understanding of subject matter to ensure that learning and teaching are in accordance with curricular requirements as stipulated by the Department for Education and Skills (DfES) and the various examination boards. Whilst much has been written about the importance of subject knowledge and applying that knowledge to the learning and teaching process, the following explains how students mediate improving subject knowledge during the course and also how they learn to apply their knowledge in the classroom – in other words, to make the 'content knowledge' meaningful to their pupils.

Starting points

Students are expected to have 'degree level (or equivalent) competence' in the subjects they are offering. However, there are no 'standard' degree courses offering identical course components across different universities, so students come to teacher preparation courses with different levels of knowledge and conceptual understanding of their subject area(s). Furthermore, there is little consensus regarding the *detail* of the body of knowledge that can be regarded as a pre-requisite for entrance to such a course. Evaluating students' subject knowledge base, in addition to monitoring the *updating* of knowledge and the *development* of subject knowledge, becomes a complex but necessary procedure that permeates any course of teacher preparation.

What you think you know, what you actually know, and what you need to learn

So how can you begin to improve your subject knowledge and thinking about your subject? As implied above, mediating subject knowledge and deepening understanding about your subject is an ongoing process as you learn to teach, even from the point of being accepted onto a course. Whilst the manner in which students seek to make improvements varies considerably, it is not (generally speaking) a solitary activity. To some extent it is a shared process in the sense that there are people with whom students may collaborate.

At the point of interview for courses, tutors usually attempt to assess the level of subject knowledge that the applicant possesses (see Chapter 1). This information is gathered through interview questions and set tasks. Tutors are thus better positioned to highlight specific areas that the applicant needs to address, and then negotiate how necessary progress can be achieved. This is not an unusual practice and prospective applicants will find it helpful to note that tutors often set pre-course reading for successful applicants to be completed prior to the start of a course. Applicants may also be advised that it is desirable for them to follow one of the Subject Knowledge Booster Courses offered in a number of institutions. These aim to improve subject knowledge in your main subject specialism, and in subsidiary subjects where offered. Some applicants work assiduously at addressing suggestions made at interview prior to the start of a course. One Science student, for example, recounted how she 'revised all summer after the interview' accumulating 'three folders of stuff'. This was not random 'stuff' however, as further conversation revealed, but the result of meticulous research based on subject knowledge required in relation to the National Curriculum, GCSE and A-level specifications. Guidance about how to structure this 'revision' (a misnomer as some of this was clearly 'new learning', we later discovered) was offered by the course tutor following initial acceptance onto the PGCE course.

Auditing subject knowledge

Once on a course, students are required by their tutors to complete *subject knowledge audits* in the subjects they will be teaching. It is common too for students to complete audits that assess their knowledge, skills and understanding relating to information and communications technology (ICT). These audits aim to make students aware of the range of knowledge and understanding they already possess, to identify the areas in which they need to develop in order to deliver the curriculum competently, and even to suggest what going beyond those boundaries might mean. In completing them, students are given the opportunity to identify areas of subject knowledge that they feel 'expert in' (a phrase used by students) and those that need to be enhanced.

What does a subject knowledge audit look like? Examples are shown in Figures 3.1, 3.2 and 3.3. The form and content of audits can vary according to individual disciplines. The range of models used can adopt tick box approaches, or may offer opportunities for you to comment on the extent to which you have appropriate subject knowledge, or they may run along the lines of a Likhert scale to indicate satisfaction or dissatisfaction with one's level of subject knowledge. Some audits are highly structured and find their form elaborated around a framework which takes account of the knowledge that needs to be develop in relation to the requirements of the National Curriculum, the topics covered in examination specifications at GCSE and A-level, and the Qualifying to Teach standards mentioned above. It is important to recognise that teachers do not have complete freedom to decide what to teach (this is defined in the curriculum), though they do have a certain amount of choice about the topics which might be covered. The majority of what pupils are expected to learn and upon which they are formally assessed is thus externally determined. Understanding frameworks such as the National Curriculum and the Programmes of Study, GCSE and vocational qualification specifications, and post-16 specifications including those concerning Key Skills, is therefore fundamental to learning about your subject. This is partly guided by the notion that on one level learning about your subject can be divided into units, though there are other considerations to bear in mind, to be discussed below. It is also usual to find in audit documentation sections requesting information about topics covered during your first degree course – in some ways the starting point for constructing the your own 'needs analysis'.

Mind the gap

Once on the UEA PGCE course, in order to address the 'gaps' in their subject knowledge audits, students engaged in pragmatic learning

UEA PGCE – MFL PARTNERSHIP

SUBJECT KNOWLEDGE AUDIT

This is an important document which once completed should be discussed at the earliest opportunity whilst on placement and reviewed regularly with your tutor and mentor. It is a working document which you will update regularly through the **PGCE** year. **Please keep a record of how you improve your subject knowledge during the year and of all supporting evidence to show progress and development.** Ensure a copy is kept in your placement file.

NAME:
How many languages do you speak and to what levels of proficiency?
Please indicate if you are a native speaker of a language other than English: YES/NO If yes, which language is your mother tongue?
Did your degree entail a period abroad? YES/NO If yes, please give details.
How confident do you feel about the languages you want to teach? Give details.
What proportion of your degree (%) was devoted to: linguistics: language work: other: (give details) literature: contemporary topics:
Which literature texts/periods did you study at university?
Which contemporary subjects did you study?
Are there any other areas of subject knowledge that you would like to inform us of?

Figure 3.1 A complete audit for a Secondary PGCE MFL course.

LANGUAGE NEEDS
Tick the boxes where you feel improvement is needed

FL 1:
- Conversational fluency
- Written language
- Listening skills
- Reading skills
- Colloquial/idiomatic language
- Grammatical accuracy
- Pronunciation and intonation
- Classroom target language
- Cultural awareness

LANGUAGE NEEDS
Tick the boxes where you feel improvement is needed

FL 2:
- Conversational fluency
- Written language
- Listening skills
- Reading skills
- Colloquial/idiomatic language
- Grammatical accuracy
- Pronunciation and intonation
- Classroom target language
- Cultural awareness

LANGUAGE NEEDS
Tick the boxes where you feel improvement is needed

FL 3:
- Conversational fluency
- Written language
- Listening skills
- Reading skills
- Colloquial/idiomatic language
- Grammatical accuracy
- Pronunciation and intonation
- Classroom target language
- Cultural awareness

LANGUAGE/CURRICULUM NEEDS
In which of the following areas do you feel you need to improve? Tick the boxes where you feel improvement is needed

FL 1:
- Knowledge about KS3
- Knowledge about KS4
- Knowledge about AS level
- Knowledge about A2 level
- Teaching grammar
- Teaching literature
- Teaching contemporary topics
- Role of the subject in the curriculum
- Knowledge about the NC for MFL
- Framework for teaching MFL
- Knowledge about MFLs as a foundation subject
- Other

LANGUAGE/CURRICULUM NEEDS
In which of the following areas do you feel you need to improve? Tick the boxes where you feel improvement is needed

FL 2:
- Knowledge about KS3
- Knowledge about KS4
- Knowledge about AS level
- Knowledge about A2 level
- Teaching grammar
- Teaching literature
- Teaching contemporary topics
- Role of the subject in the curriculum
- Knowledge about the NC for MFL
- Framework for teaching MFL
- Knowledge about MFLs as a foundation subject
- Other

LANGUAGE/CURRICULUM NEEDS
In which of the following areas do you feel you need to improve? Tick the boxes where you feel improvement is needed

FL 3:
- Knowledge about KS3
- Knowledge about KS4
- Knowledge about AS level
- Knowledge about A2 level
- Teaching grammar
- Teaching literature
- Teaching contemporary topics
- Role of the subject in the curriculum
- Knowledge about the NC for MFL
- Framework for teaching MFL
- Knowledge about MFLs as a foundation subject
- Other

Figure 3.1 (continued).

UEA PGCE – MFL PARTNERSHIP
IMPROVING SUBJECT KNOWLEDGE LOG

NAME: _____

Please use this form to log actions you take to improve your subject knowledge over the PGCE year. A copy should be kept in your placement file and it should be reviewed on a regular basis by your mentor.

Please keep a record of how you have improved your subject knowledge during the PGCE year and of all supporting evidence to show progress and development.

DATES (from . . . to . . .)	LANGUAGE	MAIN OBJECTIVE	TYPE OF LEARNING ACTIVITY	RESOURCES USED (people/places/materials etc.)	FURTHER NEEDS IDENTIFIED

Figure 3.1 (continued).

KNOWLEDGE AND UNDERSTANDING

This audit considers your subject knowledge and understanding in each of the activity areas of the Physical Education Programmes of Study and 14–19 Examinations.

> **Please enter 1, 2 or 3 in each box in relation to how confidently you can provide learning experiences at the different key stages.**
>
> 1. I feel I have **secure knowledge and understanding** to teach this activity
> 2. I feel **I need to update my subject knowledge and understanding** in order to effectively teach this activity
> 3. I am unfamiliar with this area and need to **significantly develop my subject knowledge and understanding** in order to effectively teach this activity

ATHLETIC ACTIVITIES		SEPTEMBER KS3 KS4 GCSE	MARCH KS3 KS4 GCSE	JUNE KS3 KS4 GCSE
TRACK	Sprinting			
	Middle/Distance			
	Hurdling			
	Relay			
JUMPS	Long			
	Triple			
	High			
THROWS	Shot			
	Javelin			
	Discus			
CROSS COUNTRY RUNNING				

> **Targets set with mentor(s) to address gaps in Athletic Subject Knowledge**

Figure 3.2 Extracts from a Secondary PE subject knowledge audit.

DANCE ACTIVITIES	SEPTEMBER KS3 KS4 GCSE	MARCH KS3 KS4 GCSE	JUNE KS3 KS4 GCSE
DANCE COMPOSITION			
DANCE FORMS Traditional/Cultural			
EXERCISE TO MUSIC e.g. Aerobics/Step			

Targets set with mentor(s) to address gaps in Dance Subject Knowledge

GYMNASTIC ACTIVITIES	SEPTEMBER KS3 KS4 GCSE	MARCH KS3 KS4 GCSE	JUNE KS3 KS4 GCSE
EDUCATIONAL Themes			
Floor Work			
Sequence Work			
Apparatus			
OLYMPIC			
Skills i.e. Handstand			
Vaulting			
Trampette Work			
TRAMPOLINING			

Targets set with mentor(s) to address gaps in Gymnastic Subject Knowledge

Figure 3.2 (continued).

What is your ICT quotient?

---

1. Computers: range of hardware platforms

I don't know how to use any computer hardware system **0**
I can confidently use only one computer hardware system **4**
I am confident using PC and Apple systems **10**

---

2. Computers: level of technical capability

None **0**
Very basic; I can just about get round the system but sometimes get stuck **3**
Quite confident; I know how to do most things (file management, multi-tasking,
  integrating and transferring bits and pieces from different applications) **7**
All this plus can usually reconfigure and fix the system without having to send
  for the mendy-person when something won't work **10**

---

3. Digital Cameras

I am aware of what they are **1**
I can use one **3**
I can use a digital camera to transfer pictures into other applications **7**
I use them in my teaching and preparation of lessons, on field trips etc. **10**

Figure 3.3 Extracts from a Secondary History PGCE audit for
        ICT.

4. Art packages

I know what they do **1**
I can make some sort of picture using them **3**
I am confident in using most features of art packages **6**
I can use them and am aware of how they can be used in teaching **8**
I regularly make use of them in my preparation of resources and teaching **10**

5. Voice recognition software

I know what it is **1**
I can just about use it **3**
I can use it proficiently **6**
I have used it successfully in my teaching **10**

6. Word processing

I can't word process **0**
I can do basic word processing (moving and adjusting text, saving and printing etc.) **3**
I am confident and accomplished in word processing and can do most things **5**
I can use some of the advanced features of word processors **7**
I can 'find my way' around most word processing packages **9**
I am aware of the ways in which the word processor can be used by history teachers to help to develop pupils' historical understanding **12**

Figure 3.3 (continued).

---

7. Data-handling

I don't know what data-handling is **0**
I know what it is but I don't know how to do it **2**
I know how to use a data handling package or commercially produced data file **5**
I know how to construct my own data file using a data-handling package **7**
I know what sort of questions to ask of history data files **9**
I feel confident that I could teach/demonstrate how to construct a data file to a group of students **10**
I could do all this using a variety of data-handling packages **12**
I can do all this and am confident that I could teach pupils how to use a data handling package **15**

---

8. Spreadsheets

I'm not sure what they are and what you can do with them **0**
I know what they are but don't know how to use a spreadsheet application **2**
I know the difference between a database and a spreadsheet **4**
I know how to use a spreadsheet application **6**
I know how to use spreadsheets for a variety of purposes **8**
I know how to use a range of spreadsheet applications **10**
I can use them and know ways in which history teachers can make use of them **12**

Figure 3.3 (continued).

activities which encompassed reading textbooks, specialist books and journal articles, surfing the Web for information, watching videos prepared for pupils, completing exam papers and studying the defined content for examination and syllabuses. Students also signalled that there were various learning communities which had an impact on learning about their subject. Peer learning was very common. For example, students following the Modern Foreign Languages (MFL) course developed subject knowledge through 'language lunchtimes' when a group would discuss a topical issue, or grammatical or structural point, speaking only in a given language. This involved one student with good subject knowledge preparing for the 'lesson' and leading a group of friends in conversation. This type of collaborative learning was helpful on a number of levels as students learned about the necessity of taking risks when trying to speak a language in which they did not feel proficient, and they were also able to share successful learning and teaching strategies through discussion of the methods adopted by the 'teacher' of the group.

In addition, they were improving their subject knowledge through learning more language. One MFL student commented that overall this experience of learning about their subject in an unthreatening environment (with peers) helped build their confidence before going into school for a block placement.

With regard to ICT, other students discussed learning about educational software and relevant applications through more knowledgeable peers demonstrating their use. Often this happened in an 'unplanned manner'. For example, when working in computer laboratories during lunchtimes, if students hit a problem they would seek help from more knowledgeable peers who would quickly help troubleshoot the problem. One student noted that this was how many children also learnt in computer rooms in school. Other strategies that supported such development and which were valued by students centre around more formally organised opportunities for 'microteaching' (teaching part of a lesson to their peer group) and delivering presentations to peers.

Some students spoke of the benefits of joining subject associations. These offered further opportunities to expand knowledge as related journal publications emanating from these link directly to teaching and learning in secondary schools. Students remarked that the research conducted for some of the articles encouraged them to develop a reflective approach to their work as teachers, enabling a problem-solving approach when issues related to learning and teaching surfaced in their placements. Equally, those students who joined electronic discussion groups found that within these virtual environments it was possible to locate teachers and fellow students who were able to offer advice on subject-specific issues. A number of students used these forums to request and exchange information about resources for teaching particular topics and also to discuss subject-specific methods for teaching them.

Knowledge, understanding and skills

An important theme that emerged from discussion with students about subject knowledge audits is that they are not only instrumental in indicating required knowledge and understanding in relation to subject matter, but also the types of skills that teachers might need to develop in order to deliver lessons. This is particularly the case, for example, with ICT (a more general discussion of 'skills' follows

later in this chapter). The Qualifying to Teach standards (TTA, 2003) state that students should be able to:

> use ICT effectively in their teaching. (2002: 12)

and also

> know how to use ICT effectively, both to teach their subject and to support their wider professional role. (2002: 8)

As a group, the students had all come to the course with various levels of knowledge of computers. They felt that the ICT audits were helpful in making them aware of available tools and software that could be used in the learning and teaching process. Most had a good awareness of certain software programmes but little awareness initially of the range of computer skills they would need to develop. In essence, students felt that completing the subject knowledge and ICT audits was a very 'useful' starting point therefore for coming to terms with the range and breadth of topics to be covered in a subject area. The audits, they felt, tend to give an initial overview of 'what the subject is about' and the general consensus was that they are helpful in signalling where improvement is needed on an individual basis. It was felt that opportunities to review the audits and note progress at specific periods during the year also helped to set targets for future development. In conjunction with other elements of the PGCE course, it was felt that the audits also alert students to the areas they need to 'master'. 'Mastering' new knowledge *and* skills therefore became part of the core of learning about subject.

Mastering subject knowledge

The notion of 'mastering' was a theme raised several times and by several students. It became clear that 'mastering' also has different meanings and therefore different implications for possible courses of action when learning about your subject. Above all, however, students stated that initially they felt studying the frameworks previously mentioned helped them grasp the fact that learning and teaching in English schools is very much situated, as they provide an opportunity to view the teaching of individual subjects in a sequential manner from Key Stage 3, through to Key Stage 4, then at the post-16 level, in addition to outlining the topics and concepts

to be learnt. One student stated that in a way these frameworks were a 'a relief' as 'once you get over the number of bulleted points you can begin to plan the learning for pupils – and any [learning] you need to do!' But when the statement was unpicked in the discussion, students began to speak about the complexities of working with frameworks and about a number of dilemmas they faced when learning about their subject.

On one level 'mastering' referred to being cognisant of the changing nature of subject matter. Whilst at the start of the course students stated they were conscious of the need to learn more about their subject, it is significant that students noted the degree to which it is pertinent to note that subject matter constantly 'grows and changes'. Students were careful to point out that adopting an approach which assumes there are a finite number of topics or ideas to be learnt is insufficient, and furthermore does not demonstrate an appreciation of the dynamic nature of one's subject. A Biology student noted:

> 'Biology is constantly changing and many areas I had to teach topics at A-level I had never done before – for example, cereals and enzyme technology.' (Janice)

This student went on to state that as advances are made in industry and technology, the knowledge generated becomes part of the curriculum. She drew attention to the fact that not only students but also qualified teachers need to continually update their subject knowledge as part of their professional development. Such changes have implications for teachers and how they view and react to the need to improve subject knowledge, and for how they see their subject and its application to the contextual realities of the 'world out there' beyond the school perimeter. For Janice, learning about her subject in relation to the taught curriculum became an exciting personal project, offering an opportunity to be up to date with changing technology. Given the popularity of such topical issues amongst the young people she was teaching, she felt it was a very worthwhile investment of time to develop her knowledge in this direction.

I know, therefore I teach?

On another level, 'mastering' was interpreted as the ability to question your own assumptions about your subject knowledge, and

how such self-awareness can be utilised to ensure that learning takes place in the classroom. The following quotation is typical of comments made by students in this respect:

'At the beginning of the placement I thought that teaching Science, particularly Biology, would be simple. This was not the case – teaching something you find easy to pupils can be difficult! Quite often I was thinking, "how can they possibly not understand?" I have since learned to simplify what I teach, breaking it down to a basic level.' (Malika)

Given that one of the first elements that students become aware of during initial teacher education is the importance of the quality of one's subject knowledge and its relation to effective learning and teaching, and given the frameworks within which preparation courses operate, students evidently tend to be concerned with developing a *personal* understanding of the subjects they teach. One Physical Education student, who initially found the 'space and shape' part of the curriculum 'difficult', described her subject knowledge as 'better' after further study.

'I feel confident with shape and space now. I understand the reasons behind a lot of things I felt I "just knew".' (Gillian)

The process of researching the 'reasons' and of developing a deeper understanding resulted in a more confident classroom presence for this student. The message that students took from such episodes is to question assumptions held about how well one actually knows and understands a subject and individual topics to be taught. This process of reconstructing knowledge helps to develop confidence and better prepares the student to explain concepts and principles to pupils.

Alongside that, as you begin to observe lessons and to engage in delivering lessons yourself, one question that emerges through this process of self-assessment is not only whether you possess sufficient subject knowledge, but also how it might be possible to relate that knowledge to pupils to ensure that they learn and can use the knowledge for themselves. Students stressed that it is not a 'given' that because you 'know' your subject you can teach it. Their reflections revealed that knowledge can sometimes be taken for granted, as represented through the assumptions they made

regarding understanding of the underlying principles of certain phenomena and topics they were teaching.

This point was further emphasised by students through discussion which focussed on the process of 'applying' knowledge. Here students referred to planning lessons and schemes of work. This was the moment when many begin to gain a fuller appreciation of the meaning of what it is to learn about the subject in the overall context of learning and teaching in schools. As one student said:

> *'Subject audits were helpful but no substitute for sitting down and planning a topic. I found that I thought I was familiar with a subject until I sat down to plan. Then I had to go back to the books and brush up.' (Maria)*

The dilemma facing students then became how to organise learning. Whilst students felt it was positive to know (through the specifications) the breadth and scope of their subject within the formal curriculum, and thus the key areas that they would be engaged in teaching, these are insufficient to help with the planning of schemes of work and individual lessons. Students felt that real learning about their subject lay in developing a critical and analytical capacity concerning how subject knowledge is created and how it should be organised for teaching purposes. In this case, Maria explained that although subject knowledge audits may lead students to identify topics they need to revise or learn, this has little meaning until merged into the bigger picture of planning for learning. Learning about your subject is not about 'learning in general' but about developing knowledge for a 'specific purpose' and to teach a 'specific group of youngsters'. Planning lessons requires you to have a clear conceptual framework whereby you can organise learning based on what pupils already know, and upon that which is to be learnt.

In relation to this, a number of students mentioned that when they had assumed they had sufficient knowledge about a topic they were 'lulled into a false sense of security' and became 'unstuck' when delivering lessons: pupils would ask questions to which they were unable to respond, and this left them feeling insecure. Such experiences led many to realise that it is necessary to develop a large 'mental map' of one's subject – variously described as 'challenging and daunting'! Understanding how to organise and sequence learning activities which enable pupils to progress in a logical and linked manner clearly expands the notion of what subject knowledge may be.

Other comments made by students regarding subject knowledge and understanding and planning for learning in relation to their performance in the classroom include the following:

> 'Having good subject knowledge has enabled me to be confident about what I am teaching and this improved my [classroom] performance and consequently the pupils' learning.' (Sue)

> 'I found it was less of an issue of what I knew – more of me finding out what the pupils did and didn't know. I have a good understanding of my subject and of which areas need more time or more explanation to enable pupils to make progress.' (Nick)

> 'Sometimes good subject knowledge makes it harder to pitch the language at the right level . . . I had to revise my expectations of pupils. I had to look at the scheme of work more closely and the textbooks in order to teach the pupils more effectively. I sometimes realised that I had big gaps in my lesson plans and I was assuming prior knowledge on the part of the pupils, particularly as regards grammar. I also realised that it's no good telling the pupils a word in French only once – you've got to find ways of helping them to learn that and internalise it.' (Louis – native French speaker)

It seems that the deeper the subject knowledge, the more confident students feel in their ability to plan appropriately. However, it is important to note the link made with developing and adopting appropriate teaching strategies, including a range of techniques for explaining concepts to pupils and enabling learning to take place. The majority of students believe that deeper subject knowledge and understanding helps to anticipate teaching points that potentially pupils might find difficult to grasp.

In order to enable more effective planning, Maria researched the topics to be taught through reference to textbooks, long- and medium-term schemes of work in the department in which she was completing the school-based placement, and through discussion with colleagues focussed on the learning activities which would best suit the objectives of individual lessons. Nick's strategy paid careful attention to discovering the nature of pupils' prior knowledge and to constructing lessons which allowed sufficient time to be spent on those concepts requiring more explanation and opportunities for pupils to practise using/applying these. Louis had to 'unlearn' what he already knew as a native speaker of French in order to understand the potential difficulties that non-native speakers of French would have in learning the language, and to develop activities to practise the language.

Other students pointed out that for them the process of learning about their subject encompassed an appreciation of the ways in which more secure subject knowledge enabled them to be more 'flexible' in the approaches adopted when teaching. 'Flexible' for the students signified that teaching repertoires expanded: they were less likely to plan lessons which were wholly teacher-centred and more confident about encouraging exploration, discussion and debate with and amongst pupils. As placements progressed, they generally also felt confident to move away from planned activities and to follow threads of discussions or ideas emanating from pupils, for they were not 'afraid' and 'lessons became more creative and enjoyable' – both for students and pupils – through these multiple pathways to learning. No doubt there were other factors influencing these changes in teaching styles which might include, for example, growing confidence about classroom management, more in-depth knowledge about individual pupils, and assessment (discussed in a following section). Students felt that all of these elements are interlinked.

Teaching outside your specialism

It would be helpful at this point to consider the students' experiences of improving subject knowledge in relation to teaching outside their specialist fields, be this in a second subject or in an area within their specialist subject that they have not previously learnt or were unfamiliar with. What about a Physics specialist required to teach Biology, a Spanish expert wishing to teach German, or an English specialist keen to try some Media Studies? Whilst not all students offer a second subject, a significant proportion do so, and many more would like to. Of course, many students join courses with the necessary qualifications, but in some cases there is considerable insecurity about these 'second subjects'. They might have constituted a lesser proportion of a student's degree, or may have been studied only to A-level.

One student reflected upon the fact that he felt stressed and unprepared at the start of his first school-based placement because of his lack of subject knowledge. The following is typical of the sorts of comment students made about their second subjects:

> '*Teaching GCSE Physics was challenging. Having not studied Physics since secondary school, I had to spend time learning the topics myself. This learning was supported by the teacher whose lessons I was taking. Once I had become confident with the content of the lessons, I was able to relax and they were amongst my most successful lessons.*' *(George)*

This excerpt is very telling about the psychological and physiological effects that can result from feeling insecure about subject knowledge. George went on to explain that he was only able to 're-lax' once he had developed an understanding of the central concepts of the topics he was teaching (even though this was at a basic level when compared with his first subject offering). There were a number of reasons for this. He feared pupils asking questions to which he did not know the answer (also mentioned above). He wanted to appear to have 'expert knowledge' although he acknowledged that at some stage pupils were bound to ask a question for which he would not have the answer, even in his first subject offering. The underlying belief for George was that expert knowledge would help him to establish himself in the role as teacher and therefore make it more likely that he would earn the respect of his pupils. In addition, George stated that developing his subject knowledge enabled him to plan his lessons in a logical manner, moving from simple to more complex ideas and also to map his understanding of the subject in such a way as to integrate appropriate learning activities for the pupils. This for him was how 'the most successful lessons' were generated. In developmental terms, George had clearly recognised from his first experiences of being in the classroom that he needed to identify how much he knew about the subject and then to build upon this to ensure that his own confidence developed. He also quickly grew to appreciate that this was not significantly different from what he felt about teaching his first subject. As the reader will recognise, George's story is not so different from the experiences described earlier but does perhaps vary somewhat in terms of the intensity of what he felt.

What may be of particular interest to those planning to teach more than one subject is that some students discussed the need to develop different teaching styles for each subject taught. A history student noted:

> *'I taught Art, but the challenge was not in terms of subject knowledge but it was because I had to totally change my teaching style.' (Ruby)*

Whilst it has already been noted elsewhere that learning about your subject is closely associated with the need to learn about subject methodology, this takes on another dimension when teaching more than one subject.

Learning about your subject is about understanding the most effective ways of teaching individual subjects and about how pupils learn that particular subject. Students were keen to stress that learning about your subject must also include learning about other subjects in the curriculum. It is worthy of note that whilst there are differences in the approach to teaching and learning in individual subject areas, there are also similarities. One of the most significant learning moments that students mentioned related to the discovery (through interactions and discussions with peers from different subject areas during the Professional Development seminars based at the university) that there are also many generic skills that all teachers are endeavouring to help pupils develop, and several cross-curricular links to be made between different subject areas. The notion of training to be a teacher of a particular subject area therefore became less dichotomous for some. Through these seminars students learnt more about how their subjects are conceptualised and framed by others. Some students noted that individual subjects can be stereotyped and/or valued in different ways by their peers. For some students, this led to deep reflection about why their subject features in the curriculum, the extent to which it features as compulsory or optional foundation subject, and the politics involved in specifying what should be taught in schools, to what level and within what timeframe.

Learning about pupils' knowledge

On a lighter but nevertheless serious note, students also stressed that learning about a subject was also about understanding what pupils know and believe about different subject areas, their lack of knowledge, and their preconceptions and misconceptions. Sometimes students were amused by statements made by pupils, and at others horrified. Here are just a few examples cited by students when discussing their own lessons:

1. *Pupil: Hormones are contraceptives.*
2. *Pupil: Plants eat soil.*
3. *Pupil: Plants eat light.*
4. *One year 7 pupil thought instead of flowing through veins and arteries, our blood sloshes around our body – effectively making us big bags of blood!*
5. *Pupil: All Christians are evil (RE lesson).*
6. *Pupil: PE is not important. It's time to have a mess about.*
7. *Mr H: Josh, why do you think that your textbook is a more reliable piece of evidence than the one written by the monk at the time of the Peasants' Revolt?*
   Josh: Because my textbook is the truth.

Whilst the students said they had considered the importance of pupils' prior learning when planning lessons, they sometimes felt surprised by the lack of knowledge that pupils demonstrated, the views and beliefs held by some and the undervaluing of their subject areas. Whilst it can sometimes be relatively easy to correct factual misunderstandings that pupils have (1–4 above), students stressed that learning about their subject encompassed also the complex nature of ethical dimensions of teaching and learning. Students felt that it is necessary to consider how to respond thoughtfully to pupils so as to foster appreciation of all subject areas and enable pupils to develop 'enlightened attitudes'. Such episodes were amongst the most challenging for students, yet were powerful in helping students adopt reflective approaches to the their subject areas.

Knowing about assessment

An integral part of learning about your subject encompasses developing an understanding of assessment. Some students stated that they came to the course thinking that they knew about its purposes: this was based on their own experiences of being pupils and students at university. However, as they learnt more about different ways of assessing pupils and also about the role of the teachers in that process, they were overwhelmed by its complex nature.

The expectations of what and how teachers should monitor and assess pupils is outlined in Section 3.2 of the Qualifying to Teach standards (TTA, 2003). This document requires students to learn how to use a range of monitoring and assessment strategies, to use such information to inform planning, to provide feedback to pupils, to involve pupils in evaluating their own progress, to use nationally established frameworks for assessing progress, to guide the improvement of children of all abilities and needs, to record progress systematically and to report pupils' progress to parents and other professionals.

Ways into understanding monitoring and assessment of pupils involved a number of activities. All students stated that during taught sessions at the university they were engaged in activities which allowed them to consider the National Curriculum Attainment Targets (ATs) criteria, Key Stage 3 tests, GCSE, AS and A2 marking criteria. Some 'sat' the examinations in order experience what the process was like in addition to testing their subject knowledge, and all had engaged in marking examination work as well as class work using either the attainment target criteria or mark schemes for other specifications. Students felt that it was through the marking of pupils' work in particular and using specified marking criteria that they learnt much about how to organise learning and teaching in their subject area.

Most students, however, found it challenging to work with the criteria:

> *'They seem really well presented and even logical when you first read them. But then you get this piece of work to mark and those criteria don't seem to mean very much anymore!' (Louis)*

Marking criteria may seem clear given their orderly presentation, but if we take the National Curriculum Attainment Targets as an example, the level 5 criteria of the Listening and Responding section for Modern Foreign Languages requires pupils to:

> . . . show that they understand extracts of spoken language made up of familiar material from several topics, including present, past and future events. They cope with language spoken at near normal speed in everyday circumstances that has little

or no interference or hesitancy. They identify and note the main points and specific details, including opinion and may need some repetition. (DfEE, 2000: The National Curriculum Attainment Targets, p. 37)

In this example, students felt that there were numerous potential challenges in applying the criteria as it was possible to interpret it in a number of ways. What exactly are 'familiar materials'? How many topics would constitute 'several topics' – three, six or eight? What speed is 'near normal speed'? Would the slurred speech of a tipsy French speaker count as acceptable? Furthermore, students' concern turned to the construction and availability of suitable assessment materials: where would you find the tipsy French speaker for pupils to listen to?

The ways in which students were helped to learn how to apply marking criteria and address similar concerns were many. Mentors and other teachers worked with students to explain agreed understanding of how some of the more nebulous criteria statements are interpreted within individual departments. Students participated in marking pieces of work against the criteria and comparing the level they awarded with those of more experienced staff. Such strategies were found helpful by students as they offered opportunities to have a dialogue about specific issues concerning not only the National Curriculum Attainment Targets, but also the criteria for national examinations, thus helping to build an understanding of progression within and across the key stages of learning. Students also routinely engaged in observing teachers marking in situ in speaking tests for Modern Foreign Languages and English, and when assessments were made in dance and gymnastics lessons in Physical Education.

Another area of tension that students noted centred around pupils' lack of knowledge of the criteria against which they are assessed. Whist working with the criteria is important for teachers, it is equally important that pupils understand what is required of them, how their work is judged, and also how they can improve against the set criteria. Many students took time to re-word marking criteria in 'pupilspeak' and where these already existed in their departments, to look at examples of how marks would be awarded and make explicit the type of knowledge and skills that they have to demonstrate.

Through discussions and opportunities to learn about assessment from teachers and tutors, students also gained an understanding of the importance of planning in relation to 'planning for learning'. The inter-relatedness of assessment and planning struck trainees as commonsensical in initial theoretical discussions on these topics. However, how to connect the two areas proves more challenging! Through consideration of assessment criteria, students felt they were better able to attempt the construction of teaching plans based on the articulation of clearer aims and learning outcomes. They were also able to consider the nature of their subject from both a skills base and content base, and from this, make judgements about which teaching styles were more likely to promote learning.

The diagnostic element inherent in tracking progress was also an area that students felt was developed through practical opportunities to mark work. Teachers are required not only to make professional judgements about what pupils have achieved but also to offer pupils constructive formative feedback to facilitate further improvement. Such action depended on the student having thorough and accurate knowledge of how the marking scale progresses and what is expected at each stage in order to discuss pupils' achievements and areas for improvement. Furthermore, students also noted the need to praise pupils in order to encourage improved future outcomes. Through this learning process students became sensitive to the requirement to balance the needs of individuals and the class as a whole. In the process of providing feedback to pupils, it was possible to assess their own performance as teachers and whether or not teaching aims had been achieved, or whether it was necessary to revisit certain topics. The tension resulted when there might be a need for some pupils to revise a topic but time for others to move on. This led students to develop the ability to differentiate the learning activities they set up so as to accommodate individual pupil needs through the cyclical process of planning, assessing students and reviewing progress made.

A point worthy of note here is that whilst students felt assessment was part of a cycle also involving planning, teaching and reflection and teaching, some developed a deep-seated wariness of the effect that assessments and examinations can have both on pupils and on students. One student noted:

'I found pupils more concerned with meeting requirements of exams rather than developing subject knowledge. For example, a GCSE top set wanted to know why we studied ten poems for

an anthology when the exam question only required them to answer about two! My argument that studying all the poems would broaden their understanding and were worth studying purely because they were interesting was, I think, a bit lost on them.' (Ali)

This backwash effect (given the current culture of assessing and examining pupils at several intervals in their school career) is not surprising and there are real dangers in adopting a 'teach to test' regime. Most students stated they wanted to teach pupils about all aspects of their subject areas and to try to encourage them to enjoy learning the subject as much as they do. Given that assessments and examinations can limit rather than enhance the learning and teaching process, students began to appreciate the importance of developing assessment tools which formed 'an everyday part of lessons' and which were 'less intrusive'. This led some to reconsider the purposes of the assessments they set when planning and their timing. Amongst the variety of methods employed to track pupils' progress were video and audio recordings of discussions and debates, project work portfolios and exhibitions.

Conclusions

Through having considered the experiences of students in learning about their subject, it is possible to extrapolate certain approaches which might be useful to you if you are considering a course in preparing to teach, or just beginning a programme. Students who have already worked through the process first and foremost stress the need for thorough subject knowledge in relation to the frameworks within which they will operate as secondary school teachers. In addition, there is acceptance that learning about your subject is a layered and simultaneous act whereby you learn about subject matter alongside your teaching of that subject matter. Within this you need to consider how pupils learn, how much they already know and how best to ensure progression in learning through planning appropriate activities, and developing and using appropriate materials. It is also important to reflect upon the contexts in which knowledge about your subject can be developed during your initial teacher education course: as has been ascertained, there is a complementarity of learning which students undertake on their own, as a result of guidance from tutors and peers, in school with help from teachers, and through the act of teaching and listening carefully to pupils. Being conscious of all these elements is likely to help you develop approaches to learning about your subject. However, what is clear is that that all students have very different experiences of the process, and it is for this most of all that you should be prepared.

Chapter 4

Learning through observing

Sue Cramp

This chapter considers how observation of other teachers at work can help you learn about teaching and about pupils. At first it may seem easy – as if it is no more than sitting and watching. However, you will soon find that it can be difficult initially to know what to look for, or that there are actually too many things on which to concentrate! The students commenting here explain how observation benefited them, and how they set about it.

The influence of your own teachers – recollected observations

Learning through observation begins with your own experience of school. A student teacher said of one of their own teachers:

> 'She is certainly someone who has inspired me to join the teaching profession and I hope that I can have the same effect on someone else one day.'

Think back to your own teachers. Identifying the characteristics you valued as a pupil can help you to develop a picture of a successful teacher, the sort of teacher you may wish to become. Students are encouraged to do this at the beginning of many teacher preparation courses. Some of the most frequent responses they give are about the atmosphere generated in the classroom by the teachers they knew at school:

> 'She inspired the class to work together and to be a "family" when we were with her. She was quick to praise and the

comments she wrote when the books had been marked gave us a sense of pride and achievement.'

'He had an enthusiasm which started with his subject but seemed to fill the whole room.'

Many identify the preparation and energy they observe in good teachers, but also show an awareness that the many responsibilities of teachers – often beyond classroom teaching – can impact on quality of teaching and relationships with pupils:

'She was always prepared for the lesson and had masses of energy, enthusiasm and resources to help us.'

'She was always very enthusiastic about her subject and this clearly rubbed off on the pupils. She made the effort to make learning fun through active participation.'

'Unfortunately when he [gained promotion] his teaching declined, he was late for lessons or would have to leave early … ultimately he lost respect with the class.'

Entering the profession with these ideals you will very quickly discover how time spent in preparing lessons and the energy expended in the classroom mean that teaching is both physically and mentally exhausting. However, the rewards from responsive pupils can far outweigh the costs of your time and energy.

In their recollections of their own teachers, students also highlight the need for good teachers to have high expectations of their pupils:

'What I appreciated most was that he set high standards and treated us like adults – stretching us in every lesson. This was not the norm in my school, as some of the teachers approached mixed-ability groups with a "lowest common denominator" pitch in mind. It is interesting looking back and seeing how many of us rose to the challenge when we were pushed.'

Early observations: setting your own goals and expectations

Having thought back to your own teachers, you need to begin the process of developing your own teaching style. Many initial preparation courses begin with some observation time in primary and secondary schools. These observation opportunities allow you to begin the process of becoming a teacher and can confirm for you that you have made not only the right choice of career, but also chosen the schooling phase to which you feel most suited:

> 'Comparing primary and secondary makes you realise you want to teach secondary.'

> 'During my observations in both the primary and secondary schools which I visited, I have been able to see school life from the "other side", i.e. from a teacher's point of view as opposed to the pupil's point of view – these were two somewhat different views.'

One student became very involved in these initial observations and although he found the experience exhausting he was able to see that this was, for him, the beginning of his development as a teacher:

> 'The observation before the course started was very helpful, but very tiring. It gave me an insight (in general) to the rules and routines involved in school. It is very surprising how tiring observation is, but it allowed me to develop ideas of what type of teacher I wanted to be.'

Another identified the value of these early observations in terms of setting up expectations, remarking that the observation period offered:

> 'a good introduction to a teaching career, as I was able to see what was really expected of a teacher.'

Later in the course you will find that observations give you the opportunity to reflect on your own teaching and to adapt your practice as a result:

> 'Later I put more observations of classes into practice – they did influence the kind of lessons I gave, what and how I got the class to work, how and when to change pace and activity based on what I observed of the group with their regular teacher.'

The art of observing teachers

'I think the initial observations quickly set up expectations in your own mind about how you feel you would teach the pupils. By doing this you begin a sort of dynamic self-evaluation that lasts the whole course. You begin to question how you will interact with everybody you meet and teach and work alongside.'

This 'dynamic self-evaluation' is an essential part of becoming a reflective teacher. This process does not always come easily. Many students felt supported in these early observations by using targeted observation sheets (see Figure 4.1), a feature of many initial teacher education programmes:

'The observation sheets provided were very useful as when you start, you do not know exactly what to observe.'

However, a few students noted that in the early stages of the course they didn't know what they should be observing and felt that their time in school was rather wasted for this reason:

'I needed more of a focus for observations. At the beginning I didn't know what to look for in lessons.'

Later in the course these same people were able to identify that they could see value in observing. Lack of experience is often cited as the reason for not gaining from initial observations, so it would seem sensible to undertake as much background reading as possible before the beginning of the course and to gain as much experience as possible working voluntarily with young people. Both these experiences will give a better understanding of the demands of a teacher and help to focus your observations.

In the early observation period and at the beginning of first teaching placement you will be looking for ideas which will help you in the classroom. At this stage in teaching you will probably find that your focus is on yourself and how you will manage in the classroom:

'I was mainly looking for tips – subject approaches and class-room management'

Supplementary Guidance for Observation Tasks

Primary Observation

1. **Literacy and numeracy are core skills that have a bearing on all subject specialisms. Observe an individual pupil (or small group of pupils) over a series of lessons or a day. Describe the range and balance of literacy and numeracy activities experienced by the pupil(s) over this time, and the demands they make on the pupil(s).**

   If you are able to make detailed links with your secondary specialism you should do so.

   - Try to speak with the class teacher to see if they can suggest a pupil or small group of pupils that may be interesting to observe over the course of the day. It may also help to learn a little about the pupil(s).

   - It might help to draw up a time-chart, observing the engagement of the pupil(s) with activities every ten minutes or so, making a brief note at each interval. This leaves you chance to observe other aspects of learning in the classroom.

   - Try to get a sense of the attitude of the pupil(s) to tasks, e.g. which they find hard, which they enjoy, and try to account for this.

   - Do some literacy and numeracy skills seem to be taken for granted? Which are addressed explicitly by the teacher or other adults in the room?

   - You may find you are able to classify the activities in a manner of your own choice.

   - Which activities are best handled in pairs or groups rather than on an individual basis?

   - Which skills being developed are most pertinent to those fostered in your own subject area?

2. How are resources organised to support pupil learning?

   - The resources to be organised are numerous. They include equipment, the learning space (e.g. gym, field, classroom), presentational devices (e.g. whiteboard, screen, television), computers, books, tables, chairs. Comment on what seems interesting, novel or important.

   - The surrounding environment may be important. Do pupils have to interact with displays or the space around them as part of the lesson?

   - How are resources organised safely?

   - To what extent are pupils involved in the organisation of the resources?

   - How does organisation of resources relate to the behaviour of pupils or their motivation to learn?

   - How does the choice of resources relate to the learning intended?

Figure 4.1 Focussed observation sheets for initial primary and secondary school visits.

You may also find it helpful to visit the following websites that relate to the primary school curriculum:

http://www.standards.dfes.gov.uk/primary/
http://www.standards.dfes.gov.uk/primary/literacy/
http://www.standards.dfes.gov.uk/primary/mathematics/

Secondary Observation

1. **How do teachers typically structure lessons in your subject area?**

    You may find a table along the lines of this one helpful for gathering notes during the course of observation.

Specific examples of:	Beginning of lesson	Transitions from one activity to another
what the teacher does		
what the teacher says		
what the pupils do		

    - How do teachers start a lesson?
    - Are lesson objectives introduced? If so, how?
    - How do teachers get pupils to start an individual or series of tasks?
    - What types of activity appear to create most problems for a) the teacher and b) the pupils?
    - How are group activities set up and managed?
    - How is time distributed, and momentum created and maintained?
    - What factors seem to influence the working atmosphere in the classroom?
    - How do teachers conclude a lesson?
    - What role do resources play in structuring the lesson?

    Suggested reading:
    Scott Baumann, A., Bloomfield, A. and Roughton, L. (1997)
    Becoming a Secondary School Teacher. London: Hodder & Stoughton.
    See Ch. 17 'Planning, Preparation and Presentation'.

2. **With reference to two lessons (each representing a different key stage) that you have observed in your subject area, how do you ascertain that pupils are learning?**

    It is often difficult to see that pupils have made progress in learning. Sometimes they may not appear to learn exactly along the lines of stated learning objectives, but this does not discount the possibility that they have learnt other things. Often their learning may be something other than 'subject knowledge'.

Figure 4.1 (Continued).

- What evidence can you draw on to say that a pupil has or hasn't made progress in learning?
- Could you make a distinction between progress in knowledge, understanding and skills?
- What do pupils' answers to questions reveal about their learning? Do pupils ask questions themselves?
- What can pupils' mistakes or misconceptions tell you about their level of understanding?
- To what extent can whole-class question-and-answer phases provide a good indication of everybody's progress?
- How do you gauge progress and learning during pair or group work?
- How do you set about considering learning in activities that do not leave a record or product, written or otherwise?
- Are some forms of evidence of learning favoured over others? Are some more valuable?
- Have you witnessed any instances where it is problematic to ascertain whether or not learning occurred?

3. **With reference to the practice of the teachers you have observed, what sort of teacher would you like to become?**

   In considering your response here, we would like you to bear in mind a variety of teachers, and of course your own personality. The teacher you become will no doubt be unique, not a direct imitation of any single example!

   - Have you seen skills you would like to emulate?
   - Would you bring to your teaching anything you haven't seen?
   - What values do you want to embody or represent?
   - Will you differ from class to class?
   - What makes a good colleague?

   Suggested reading:
   Moon, B. and Mayes, A.S. (eds) (1994)
   Teaching and Learning in the Secondary School. Milton Keynes: Open University.
   See Ch. 13 'What Makes a Good Teacher?'

4. **On the basis of your experience so far, how would you advise others to approach observing learning and teaching?**

   We ask this question because observation can be difficult!

   - What were the difficulties you experienced, and how did you respond to them?
   - How did you decide where to look, and when?
   - To what extent did you switch between observer and participant roles?

Figure 4.1 (Continued).

- Did observing pose any ethical questions?
- What are the benefits of having focussing prompts, and what are the disadvantages?
- How has your experience of schools before this period of observation influenced your approach and the manner of your response?

Suggested reading:
Wragg, E. (1994) *An Introduction to Classroom Observation*. London: Routledge.
See Ch. I 'An Introduction to Classroom Observation'.

Figure 4.1 (Continued).

'I observed lots of good practice and tried to use parts of this to develop my own individual style.'

'Observing my mentor and other class teachers helped me develop my own classroom management and teaching styles.'

But at some stage during this placement your focus will move away from yourself and towards the pupils:

'During my first placement, observation became much easier and structured, and I was able to see beyond the teaching methods and into how the pupils were learning.'

Later in the year you will find that observation continues to be important. There will be a further shift of emphasis and focus, which will enhance the quality of your observations. The following comments were made during the second half of the UEA PGCE course:

'Observing other teachers on second placement is probably the most important part of our learning through others – by now we know what to look for, know areas we need to develop and can focus observations on teachers who excel in these areas.'

'Observations were more focussed on my part. Confidence was no longer an issue so I was able to focus more on subject knowledge, differentiation, teacher–pupil interaction, etc., than on more general classroom management techniques.'

Looking back at the end of the year, students were able to reflect on the value of observing other teachers:

> 'Observations are far more useful when you have taught the class because you know who the troublemakers are and who asks questions. When I first observed I looked for teacher movements, etc., because I had read the books.'

> 'It's interesting to see that the teacher has to focus on the same things as you do.'

> 'As you have more experience, you look for different things than you did before.'

> 'This was probably the most beneficial observation I did. Watching members of staff teach, having done it myself, was good as you could compare their performance with what you might have done. I knew what to look for!'

> 'These [later observations] were much more focussed on my part. They are still very rewarding and valuable and will hopefully continue in my newly qualified teacher induction year.'

> 'Since securing my job for September and nearing the end of placement, I have tried hard to try new ideas and observe other members of staff within the school. This has enabled me to become much more reflective in my own teaching and has sparked off new ideas to try in the future!'

Observing teacher–pupil relationships

Your own school experiences will mean that you can identify the need to keep a measured distance from your pupils whilst at the same time showing an interest in their development. This may be particularly important if you are joining initial teacher education immediately following a first degree – it is possible that you may be only a few years older than some of the pupils you will teach. If you are a parent the friendships you have with your own children and their friends are not necessarily appropriate in the classroom, so adjustments are necessary for you too.

Thinking back to their own experiences, students highlighted the support their teachers gave without being over-friendly:

'He didn't mess about in lessons trying to be our friend, as several other teachers did. He treated us as intellectual equals and responded to our enthusiasm with redoubled enthusiasm of his own.'

'I think he was my best teacher because he gave me confidence in myself and not just academically but more generally in the class.'

And students were also able to identify that pupils have problems relating to teachers. Children are naturally inquisitive and will want to know as much as they can find out:

'By watching one pupil I learned not to be too friendly as he had a problem defining teacher from friend, resulting in a lax classroom attitude.'

It is worthwhile deciding what you will discuss with your pupils and what rightly remains private. In most schools it is not appropriate to tell pupils your first name or discuss the more intimate details of your private life. It is certainly inappropriate to meet pupils on their own outside of the school whatever reason they may give for wanting to meet with you. You should also be aware of the dangers of being on your own with a pupil in a classroom or office. Take precautions such as leaving the door wide open or making sure that other pupils or staff are in the same room.

Though such caution is necessary to maintain pupil respect and to avoid compromising your own professional integrity, you will need to develop positive working relationships with your classes. Observing good teachers you will notice that they use a lot of praise and that their body language is neither over-friendly nor threatening.

And just in case you were thinking that forging relationships with your pupils was becoming over-serious:

'I observed a "wacky" Science teacher who walked over the desks and did ballet-style stretches over her legs whilst they were up on a table. The pupils loved her. She brought her lessons to life and had ultimate control over the class. It made me realise that you don't have to be in strict control and that a

sense of humour is important in helping create an environment that pupils can learn in.'

Observing classroom management strategies

Discipline is a frequently occurring theme throughout students' responses. At the beginning of the course you will probably be concerned about your own ability to develop a good relationship and control a class in order to create a positive working environment:

'One aspect of teaching that particularly scares me is discipline.'

You may have the opposite view, however, wondering why the lessons you observe are not as quiet and well-controlled as you would like if you were teaching. This student notes that her attitudes changed once she was in front of a class:

'I remember watching lessons and thinking that if I was teaching that lesson I certainly wouldn't allow pupil X to chat as much – then getting up in front of a class and realising that you are controlling 24 pupil Xs! It puts teaching and discipline into perspective!'

Although discipline will be one of your major concerns in the early stages of your teaching, you will soon realise that classroom management is a skill to be developed:

'Observing my mentor on first placement, I was struck that a great deal of classroom management was to do with experience and reputation – and that made me less worried about it as I knew it was something that I could develop in.'

The need to be fair and decisive was highlighted many times:

'She was a funny little thing, five foot nothing. Although she ruled the classroom with a rod of iron you always felt that she was fair. To be caught was never an injustice, just a fair cop.'

'What I also think is important is that you knew where you stood with her – behaviour was very important but you were

allowed to have fun too, in the right circumstances.'

Through observations you will identify a set of strategies which will work for you and your classes:

'You observe different class management techniques. This was a good basis on which to decide my own way of handling pupils.'

'The most successful teachers ensure that they are prominent throughout the lesson so that when they speak they are clearly the centre of attention.'

'When a pupil was reluctant to do work and was potentially disruptive, the class teacher was firm and reacted to the situation in a calm manner. The pupil then produced a good piece of work. This taught me how to deal with similar situations and that the calm approach works better than losing your temper.'

And there are some that you will decide not to use!

'The teacher who shouted all the time taught me to curtail my own shouting.'

'The teacher was really aggressive in his manner of discipline when a pupil was late. This sparked off a lot of bad behaviour on behalf of the pupils who did not respect the teacher.'

Perhaps one of the most important things to note is the importance of knowing your pupils well and treating them as individuals:

'Successful teachers treat pupils as individuals and in doing so gain pupils' respect. This helps to overcome/counteract disaffection.'

One of the major benefits of continuing your observations when you are teaching whole classes is that you realise that you are not alone in working through these concerns. Reflecting on your experiences allows you to make progress:

'On first placement self-evaluation and self-questioning is at its most intense. Observing behavioural problems and how other

teachers react to them gives you insight into something most have never had to deal with before. In this sense observation is incredibly useful.'

Observations of teachers dealing with difficult situations gives you confidence and an understanding that you will not get perfect discipline at all times:

'Perhaps the most important thing I gained from observing well-established teachers is that they still have problems with some pupils. On placement this helps you along to see that you are not the only one finding a class or pupil difficult.'

'Observing a variety of teachers and talking with them afterwards also demonstrated that even experienced teachers have bad days, or do things in a way I wouldn't. I observed the Head of Department lose control of a group of year 10s. The conversation afterwards boosted my confidence and reassured me that this is a learning process.'

Initially you may not see the benefits of observing classes outside of your own subject. However, as you gain in experience you will find that there are many benefits in observing teachers working in other departments. One student notes that:

'Observation to start with is more focussed on how topics are taught. Observations in other subjects helps you to focus on classroom management.'

Another found that observing a teacher with a similar style helped them to develop a wider range of strategies for dealing with a difficult class:

'On second placement I was having problems 'cracking' a difficult class. I chose a teacher with a similar personality to me (I think) to observe to get ideas. This was one of the most helpful influences I had.'

You will observe that it is important to set expectations and consequences for not complying. One student realised the importance of being decisive:

'Those teachers who make definite statements of intent and instantly follow them through appear to command respect.'

It is very easy to assume that classroom control is all about behaviour management. Your observations may suggest that this is not the case. If you can manage the resources in the classroom so that they are not a distraction for the pupils, then this will be one of the first steps to creating an attentive atmosphere. A Mathematics student tells us how he learnt to get his pupils to put down all their pens and equipment so that they were not distracted by fiddling with things:

'While observing a CDT teacher when I first came I noticed that she had tools and things to deal with. To make sure that everything is put down she said, "show me your empty hands." Ever since then I've used "jazz hands".'

The transitions between different parts of your lesson are equally important. If you can manage these smoothly, with pupils knowing exactly what is expected of them, then again you have made steps towards creating a positive working atmosphere:

'The better teachers are explicit and leave no room for ambiguity.'

One student gave a list of strategies she had learnt from observing other teachers:

- *Repeat certain key phrases/ways of saying phrases.*
- *Set clear targets with time limits.*
- *Manage entry/exit of pupils from your classroom.*
- *Count equipment in and out.*
- *Let children do jobs for you.*
- *Wandering amongst the class whilst talking or after setting a task gives a sense of authority. You can talk to individual groups and appear more approachable.*
- *Always keep calm, even when annoyed, and act as if the classroom is your space and you are in control.*
- *Nail problems from the start.*
- *Speak calmly and appropriately to children.*

- *Tell the pupil off for their behaviour. Do not criticise the actual person.*
- *Most importantly, respect the pupils and they will respect you.*

And, perhaps surprisingly, one student discovered very early on that 'pupils don't enjoy wasting time', which means that the majority of the class are on your side when you are attempting to create an orderly working atmosphere in the classroom. Remember not to take things personally, that the pupils are not deliberately setting out to make life difficult for you. There are many factors such as home background or disagreements with friends which will affect the way pupils behave in your lessons. As one student noted:

> *'Pupils' attitude to the class has a lot to do with uncontrollable factors (for example, weather, time of day ...) and the better teachers realise this and adjust activities accordingly.'*

Classroom management is also about how you behave in the classroom. As you learn to pitch the lesson at the right level you will find that the pupils are more responsive. Observation can help with this:

> *'It's only through experience that one can learn the language, tone and gestures appropriate to different year groups. Watching helped me adjust my expectations to a more appropriate level.'*

You also need to make sure that you engage pupils in all parts of the lesson by making sure that what you have to say is delivered in an interesting way which involves the pupils:

> *'Hands are useful for animating whatever you're saying. One teacher taught me this (not intentionally, I just observed this). If you expect the children to look at you for any length of time you need to have a certain charisma. Just like your voice can't be monotonous if you wish to engage the children ...'*

> *'Where I saw a class that I was teaching with a different teacher who had a very calming influence on them, I realised that I needed to pitch my voice better.'*

> *'She was always very enthusiastic about her subject and this*

clearly rubbed off on the pupils. She made the effort to make learning fun through active participation.'

Classroom management is also about the content and structure of your lessons:

'All teachers do things differently, but on the whole there seemed to be a beginning, middle and end to each lesson.'

'During the first observation weeks I observed a French teacher who really inspired me to involve the pupils in lessons. Pupils were involved in working the cassette recorder, leading the games at the front, explaining. The pupils were really engaged. This year I've really made an effort to involve pupils, bring them to the front, let them be the teacher for 5 minutes. This really seems to work well for the lower abilities as well.'

There is a clear link between developing positive working relationships with your classes and adapting your teaching style to your own personality and to the needs of the children. One student reflected on this as he recounted his experiences of observing a teacher in the school he attended as a pupil:

'He always came across as caring and very knowledgeable, every lesson being kept interesting. Although very quietly spoken he always kept good order in the classroom (and still does despite some quite unruly elements). I did wonder over the years how someone so "nice" and quiet commanded such respect among the pupils when other more authoritarian figures had little or none.

When I went back to my old school for observation he pointed out several of the other staff with different teaching styles whom I spent some time with. Although they had different styles, what came across was an underlying concern about the pupils' welfare, which the pupils seemed to pick up and respond to.

Whenever he asked a question he looked beyond the sea of raised hands to encourage a quieter/less-confident child to answer. If they didn't know the answer he helped them to find it through logical thinking. It didn't matter if they got it wrong, he explained it in more detail and didn't make them feel stupid.

> *The children were eager to learn and responded well to his style of teaching. He encouraged interaction and focussed always on the positives, through the use of a "praise more than criticise" approach.'*

Once you begin to engage with the individual pupils in your classroom you will find a rich source of guidance for classroom management:

> *'Classroom management! "Analysing pupils" would be a better phrase to use here ... Watching who interacts with whom and who in the class has disengaged body language was very useful. When it was my turn to teach them I was then able to split up certain pupils and be more ready for those who had shown patterns of disruptive behaviour.'*

It is also important to reflect on how your pupils have changed since you first met them:

> *'Observing how certain pupils had changed and developed in a learning capacity, I began to think back to when I first observed the classes and began to watch the pupils in my own lessons. It was amazing how, just by moving one or two pupils, the whole class was more productive and engaged. This was a valuable lesson for the future – don't forget to observe the pupils when you are busy thinking about your own performance in the classroom.'*

Observing different teaching styles in action

Very quickly you will realise that teachers develop a style that works for them and their pupils:

> *'I realised that teachers all have their own unique teaching style and different pupils respond to this in different ways.'*

You will also appreciate the need to develop your own style rather than 'being a clone' of another teacher:

> *'I was privileged enough in placement to have a mentor who was regarded as the best teacher in her school and to my mind*

one of the best teachers I had ever seen. Taking over her classes was immensely difficult because she was respected by pupils. I began by attempting to adopt her style. However, it was not a complete success as aspects of her style were radically different from my own. I drew out what did suit my style (starting lessons, pace, breaking lessons into segments and so on) and found that these have greatly assisted me.'

One student who tried to copy a very dynamic teacher found that this style wasn't working for them in the classroom. Eventually they were able to say:

'I do not want to emulate anybody in the world because I know that one must be genuine otherwise people feel that it is not the true "you" who is speaking, laughing, etc. But I think that it is useful to think of all the best qualities and to behave like that as well as possible.'

The need for different teaching styles for different classes and pupils is also highlighted:

'It was only later that I realised he had honed his teaching style not just to cater for his pupils but also to accommodate the style of the poet – not just the subject – he was teaching.'

Observation of other teachers also means that you are able to:

'compare your teaching style to other teachers and behaviour techniques, so as to evaluate different techniques for future use.'

Observing pupils and the process of learning

You may first begin learning about pupils through early observations in primary schools. Many students remember their own experiences as secondary school pupils but cannot recall their time in primary school. This leads many to express surprise at the level of understanding evident in younger pupils. One student expressed it in this way:

'It was interesting to see how intelligent the primary school pupils were.'

While an English student found that this understanding of pupils' abilities transformed the way they would teach pupils in the early years of secondary schooling:

> *'It was good to see the literacy strategy in practice, it was an eye-opener to the capabilities of pupils – their range of vocabulary is quite amazing and it made me reconsider the way I would pitch myself – I think I had previously been quite patronising.'*

This leads to a consideration of what happens when pupils move to secondary school:

> *'I was particularly interested in the transition stage, i.e. how teachers prepare pupils to move up to high school and how pupils cope when they arrive at high school.'*

As you begin to develop as a reflective classroom practitioner you will begin to relate observation and theory. A Mathematics student wrote:

> *'Before the course began I started reading Holt's* How Children Fail. *The book inspired an interest in the pupils' perspectives on teaching and learning as well as a reflection on one's own experience as a learner in schools. Specifically, Holt prepared me to look for children's strategies. We all have strategies to deal with situations … Pupils are masters at avoidance. We've got to scratch the surface as a teacher, get beyond the aesthetic, the "defences" of the learner, and find out what position they take towards learning.'*

Observing pupils is an essential part of becoming a good teacher. At some stage you need to move from a concern about what you will do as a teacher to a consideration of how you will help your pupils to learn. This involves an understanding of the way they respond to different teachers and experiences. One student expressed this progress in these words:

> *'Later in the practice observing becomes more useful because your focus shifts from the teacher to the pupils and what they are learning. It helped to stand back and watch pupils to see when they responded (and how they responded) to different*

teaching styles. Seeing the same pupils in two completely different subjects (RE and Food Technology) was an eye-opener! This was invaluable because I was able to realise that different pupils relate to subjects in different ways and it is not until you actually see this in action that you begin to understand why some children are better at certain subjects.'

As you become familiar with different theories of learning you will come to appreciate them in practice. One student expressed their interest in the social constructivist theory of learning by remarking on:

'specific watching of group dynamics and interactions, how pupils speak to each other, the way pupils use each other during lessons to bounce ideas off one another.'

They were also able to identify the value of discussion in learning:

'Reflecting as an adult, I think children sometimes find it easier to learn from one another as when ideas are verbalised there is less of a barrier.'

'I've seen some excellent examples of question and answer.'

'Each pupil is very different. Pupils seem to understand this because they often turn to each other for support.'

Another noted the need for different resources as you respond to individual needs. A science student highlights this:

'Each pupil is different. One conscientious pupil was not very dexterous. His first attempt at hand-drawing a line graph took him the whole lesson, five sheets of graph paper and two pencils. When the teacher sat him in front of a computer to draw the graph there were no more problems. He even analysed the graph in front of the class.'

An important part of this process of learning how pupils learn is following a pupil or class for a day, paying particular attention to the way in which they respond to different subjects, teachers, and environments. One important factor is the way in which pupils themselves articulate experiences. How can you as a teacher build on these, or apply insights gained from one instance in other contexts, with other classes? A Science student described the way in which pupils created their own analogy for what they witnessed one particular lesson:

> 'A very low ability group made a Science lesson more fun by suggesting that the piece of magnesium in a reaction was a leg and the acid molecules were piranha fish. They even suggested the idea that the gas given off by the reaction would be similar to the piranhas having wind.'

For you as a teacher, such analogies provided by pupils are a gift: where you feel they do accurately convey ideas in an interesting, clear form you can draw on them in your own teaching.

Others learned to appreciate the different experiences children have during the course of the school day:

> 'Shadowing a pupil through the course of their school day reminded me that my lesson isn't all that they have to do today!'

> 'Whilst trailing a pupil round a variety of classes I realised how potentially boring pupils' days could be – and that made me think about the importance of making my subject as interesting and enjoyable as possible to pupils.'

Observing the pupils you are going to teach can be of real value, particularly as you progress through the course. These are some of the things students said about observing classes prior to teaching them, each comment demonstrating some degree of helpful informal assessment:

> 'Observation of pupils on my second placement was very important as it was a good gauge of the abilities of the pupils and of what the standard of behaviour was.'

> 'I got to know the group before I taught them.'

> 'See the pupils you are going to teach and get familiar with their names. Observe how they work and their learning styles – very useful. As you are not the teacher, you have time and less pressure to observe them.'

'*I learnt that some pupils found it very difficult to adjust to different teaching methods instantly (in the same classroom and in the same subject) so I had to gradually introduce my own teaching styles so that pupils were responsive, for example, one class was very teacher led with no group work – pupils found group work very strange at first.*'

'*It was interesting to see how two particular pupils responded to the teacher's attention during the lesson; how their behaviour and focus on the work improved greatly when given some inter-action with the teacher. This highlighted the needs not only for learning but also for the social interaction aspects of school life.*'

'*It is important to observe the pupils you are going to teach. This gives you a much better idea of how to pitch your lessons, ability levels, and relationships within the class and towards teachers.*'

Observing to develop your own subject knowledge

Subject knowledge is more than having a degree in your chosen or related subject (see Chapter 3 for further exploration of this area). It is about being able to break the subject down so that your pupils can understand and be captivated by the processes of learning. It is about knowing what kinds of misunderstandings and misconceptions pupils have and the kind of mistakes they might make. Observing experienced teachers at work can help you consider what level of explanation is suitable for a particular group, or perhaps what sequence of presentation can help pupils come to terms with a complex topic:

'*Observing experienced teachers was an extremely rewarding experience. I gained many useful techniques and boosted my subject knowledge.*'

You may feel that you know your subject inside out and feel confident to address any question asked by a pupil. Or you may be more nervous that you will be caught out:

'*My mentor's teaching helped me realise that subject knowledge isn't always there at the surface and there are ways around not knowing an answer.*'

In fact there is always something new to learn, whatever your background might be:

> 'I observed a variety of lessons in both core and GCSE PE. This helped me develop my own subject knowledge, giving me ideas of activities as well as developing my classroom management and teaching strategies. I observed a variety of teachers, all of whom had different strengths; this helped inform my own teaching.'

> 'To observe good ideas delivered has been useful. One example was my mentor who was teaching a lesson involving the use of newspapers. This was a valuable experience when I then taught a similar lesson to a year 9 class.'

It's always useful to see how others might approach something you have taught or will teach yourself, and it is often very informative to see two or more experienced teachers teach the same topic with very different approaches.

Observing yourself and other new and beginning teachers

So far we have discussed the advantages of observing experienced teachers, but there are many advantages to observing people who are at about the same stage in teaching as yourself:

> 'I took part in peer observation of other PGCE students. It was very useful in highlighting teaching strategies I had not utilised enough.'

> 'Watching an NQT teach a low-ability class made me more realistic about "the art of the possible".'

And observation does not have to stop with other teachers and pupils. It is worth having a video made of yourself while you are teaching. Much can be gained from observing yourself:

> 'I had one of my own lessons filmed by another student. It is daunting, embarrassing and enlightening. You notice pupils you miss out in discussion. I'd recommend this to anyone.'

Chapter 5

Learning about pupils

Caroline Still

This chapter explores what you may learn about your pupils and the ways in which you learn about them. It considers how you might use this knowledge and understanding of your pupils to create a stimulating and safe working environment and how this information can have a positive impact on your development as a teacher. The comments have been selected from the responses of over sixty student teachers to a series of simple prompts, outlined in the main text, and some additional interviews.

It is clear from the responses of our student teachers that getting to know your pupils and acquiring an understanding of their subject knowledge, their misconceptions, their likes and dislikes, what can motivate or demotivate them, is paramount to successful teaching.

> *'One of the most important tools that I had to manage my classroom was knowing each pupil.'*

There is, of course, no single method to follow for effective teaching and learning. There are no hard and fast rules, or easy routes for you to follow. You will develop your own particular approach and acquire your own 'toolkit' of skills and techniques to be deployed in the classroom. However, it seems that for most, learning about pupils is the key to becoming a successful teacher.

Learning about your pupils and using that knowledge to develop a good rapport and productive working atmosphere will perhaps be one of your greatest challenges as a teacher, and certainly one of the most important. How you manage your classroom will determine the learning environment that you subsequently establish, and this will make a difference to what your pupils can achieve. Managing classrooms for effective learning is a demanding task, involving an extensive repertoire of complex skills. As a beginning teacher, you are often working within the 'unknown', which can make it even more of a challenge.

Getting to know your pupils

Learning names

The first step in getting to know your pupils is to learn their names, and it's a good idea to work on this as soon as possible. This means getting the abbreviations and pronunciations right too. You will undoubtedly make mistakes, but laugh at these and keep trying. The pupils will forgive you very readily in the first few weeks, but inevitably they will be less forgiving as time goes on. Merely pointing to the pupils you'd like to speak – or to those you want to stop talking out of turn – isn't effective. The importance of learning names is illustrated in the following comments from student teachers.

> 'It's really, really important to learn names and not just of the disruptive kids.'

> 'I'm not very good with names; I shrugged my shoulders and ignored the issue ... Problem was, I couldn't conduct question-and-answer sessions, or ask kids to give out equipment, or worst of all, control behaviour. "You at the back, please stop talking" just doesn't cut any ice.'

> 'I knew the naughty kids and the most and least able ones, but those in between were just a haze. So I could never connect with most of the class, or deal with low-level disruption because I couldn't name individuals.'

It is clear from these reflections that a sense of powerlessness was felt, that knowing the pupils' names provided a subtle but much needed control mechanism. When students were asked which techniques they found most helpful for learning pupils' names, these were the most frequently cited responses:

'Constructing a seating plan for each class, for each room was the first step I took. I tried to use names from the outset by glancing down at the plan.'

'With younger pupils I asked them to make a name card for their desk.'

'Getting pupils to raise their hands when responding during registration.'

Another frequently mentioned point was the process of 'giving back work', putting names to faces as books or papers are returned.

If you get into the habit of addressing your pupils by name whenever you speak to them, you will quickly develop a rapport. Having learnt their names, you are now in a better position to mentally file background information about individuals in your class.

Learning about individuals

Interestingly, there seems to be a marked difference between experienced teachers and student teachers regarding the amount of information they require about their pupils prior to meeting them. Almost all mentors, when questioned, stressed that other than essential medical information, they preferred to find out for themselves rather than take on the prejudices of others. Several said that at a later stage they would look up pupils' records or talk to colleagues about particular individuals. This science mentor typified most of the responses.

'I like to teach them first and look up information later. I like to meet them without any preconceived ideas. I try not to read anything about their characters that might prejudice me. I tell them [the pupils] that I don't know anything, that they are starting with a "clean slate". I didn't used to be like this. In the early days I wanted to know as much as possible about them before I met them.'

Student teachers in marked contrast seemed anxious about the pupils they were taking on and wanted to know as much as possible about their classes prior to meeting them; potential discipline problems seemed to be the biggest concern. Of the 60 student teachers questioned there were only 10 who, like the experienced teachers, said that they preferred to know little in advance.

So where would you look to acquire information about your pupils? Consulting files, departmental records and speaking to staff can help you to gather the essential background information and so build a picture of each individual. However, there are dangers if you focus on classroom behaviour, just as the mentor above suggested. Not only could the preconceptions about your pupils cause you, subconsciously, to treat them differently; you may also find that pupils can behave very differently within different lessons and with different members of staff. In contrast to student teachers, most of the experienced teachers felt that it was more helpful initially to glean information about ability rather than behaviour. This reflects the understandable concerns that beginning teachers have about classroom management.

To put data that you collect into context, it is essential that you acquire personal knowledge of your pupils. You will achieve this at one level through class activities, marking work, and through question-and-answer sessions, but talking to pupils individually can take things to another level. There will be opportunities for this when pupils are engaged in activities and you are able to circulate. However, you need to exploit out of class opportunities as well. 'Corridor moments', for example, when you might stop to speak to pupils as you pass them around the school, can be a real investment. A brief word about their form assembly or the next football match can help to build relationships, as this student teacher discovered:

> 'That extra curricular knowledge (especially about football) helped gain their respect.'

Gradually you will break down the daunting sea of faces in front of you, into individual personalities. You will eventually build up a network of relationships, of varying strengths and depths. This is an investment of time that will undoubtedly pay dividends in the future. You may have to chastise the behaviour of an individual, but the relationship that you have built with them should ensure that the issue is short-lived, and long-term grudges are thus avoided. There may be initial setbacks, just as there can be in any relationship, but be aware that what you are aiming to build will be achieved over months, not weeks:

> 'The classroom seemed a lot less scary once I got to know the kids.'

> 'I built up a good rapport with my form group. Despite having to tell them off, and having them in at lunch, they were sad to see me go. Pupils forget the bad experiences and remember the good ones more.'

> 'I was a bit nervous about telling kids off initially, but soon realised that by the next lesson they seemed to have forgotten all about it.'

It's reassuring to note that pupils rarely hold grudges!

Learning with your pupils

Extra curricular activities provide an ideal opportunity for you to get to know pupils and for pupils to learn more about you. Having a shared interest and working with pupils in a different setting can be enormously rewarding. Be warned though, this is not something that you should take sole responsibility for as a beginning teacher. Assisting is fine, but you would be best advised to save your energy and time for your classroom teaching in the early stages of your career. Sharing your enthusiasm for example in music, hill walking, football or chess not only allows you to discover more about the pupils, but it also enables them to have a better understanding of you. The fact that you are a relatively normal human being can sometimes come as quite a revelation! Perhaps more subtle than this are instances where your role changes to that of a fellow learner. Pupils may be more accomplished than you when it comes to playing the violin, or kicking a football. Learning with and from your pupils can help to move relationships on, as this student found after joining the school orchestra:

> 'It was years since I'd picked up my tuba and I was very rusty. I kept losing my place ... luckily Darren would point to the correct section on the score to keep me on track. He was a complete pain in lessons, but here I saw him in a different light,

we developed a kind of mutual respect and this did have a positive affect on his behaviour in class.'

First impressions

In every situation within the school environment you will need to retain your 'professional distance' (something we will return to later in the chapter), together with your expectations of pupil behaviour. This is equally important in more informal settings and during extra curricular activities. First, these pupils may be in your classroom next year, and second, they will inevitably talk about you with their peers! Although this is an ideal opportunity for you to establish a diverse scattering of allies throughout the school, it is also a great platform on which to reinforce your high expectations of pupil behaviour and your professionalism. This information will spread rapidly along the pupil grapevine and can be to your great advantage if you get the message right! The first impressions that you create are clearly important.

Imagine how interesting it would be to ask pupils about their first impressions of their teachers and the impact it had on them: almost certainly their remarks would not be uniformly flattering! The same is true of student teachers and the reactions they gave to their first encounters with pupils. Having been asked what surprised them most about the pupils they worked with, they offered the following:

'How small they are!'

'How much chocolate they consume.'

'They sometimes lie and try to manipulate you.'

'How loud they can talk and for how long.'

'How slow they can work and how little some pupils really want to do!'

'How much they know!'

'Just how low-ability some of the low-ability pupils are.'

'That they can't follow instructions even if you have told them twenty times and put it in writing.'

Planning for learning

Knowing what your pupils know

When planning your lessons, where do you begin? How do you know what to teach or how to teach it? How do you know what the pupils already know and what they need to know? It is clear that you need to get to know your pupils in order to plan effective lessons. You need to establish what they already know about a topic and what their misconceptions are too.

> The most important single factor influencing learning is what the learner already knows; ascertain this and teach him accordingly. (Ausubel, 1968)

The temptation is to plan for the group, rather than thinking about the class as individuals. This does not mean you need to write thirty different lesson plans, but you do need to incorporate a variety of different activities into each lesson that will draw on different styles of learning and in turn increase the opportunities to engage your pupils. You need to tailor your activities to meet the needs of the varying abilities that exist within the class. In a mixed-ability class, for example, this may mean that tasks will need to be differentiated by modifying them to engage the most and least able:

> *'The variation in a mixed-ability group can be vast.'*

> *'One of the most challenging things about preparing lessons for a new class was knowing at what level to pitch them and how much work pupils would get through ...'*

Knowing how your pupils learn

Within any group there will be different types of learners with their own needs and preferred styles of learning. For example, pupils may be visual learners, auditory learners or learn best by 'doing', that is, they prefer practical tasks to help them make sense of the world. Spending time finding out how your pupils learn best and helping them to understand the learning process can reap rewards. You will also have your own preferred learning style; the misconception is to believe that everyone else enjoys working in the same way as you do.

> *'There seems to be less of the "spoon-feeding" approach to learning in the classroom now. Kids are becoming more responsible for their own learning, which I think is a good thing. It takes more time to organise, though. You can't just stand up and "spout forth", you have to plan activities for the kids to actually do.'*

> *'Just because you have taught something, it doesn't mean that they know it, you have to know how to help them learn and understand.'*

Clearly, then, it is advantageous to involve your pupils in the learning process. So, in addition to sharing subject knowledge with your pupils you need to teach them how to learn. You will find that giving them the tools to learn is as important as imparting knowledge and skills. In fact, the early identification of what does and does not work for your pupils can help prevent the formation of a barrier to learning.

Pupils will be more motivated if they have a clear idea of what it is that you want them to achieve, how they can best achieve it and when they have achieved it. Trying to understand the learning needs of pupils and subsequently helping them to learn about themselves is a crucial part of your role as a teacher. Identification of the learning needs of your pupils will help them maximise their potential as learners and ultimately raise achievement.

Learning from others about your pupils' learning needs

Getting to know about the learning needs and different abilities of your pupils may involve others from both within the school and outside. You could gather this information from a variety of colleagues in school: subject teachers, form tutors, year heads and teaching assistants. You will certainly need to identify those pupils that have special educational needs (SEN). The Special Educational Needs Coordinator (SENCO) in school is the best person to talk to about this. Schools keep a register of all SEN pupils as well as pupils with health problems. You will need to be aware of pupils in your class that have particular learning needs, such as those pupils with dyslexia and of those who have learning difficulties due to behavioural problems, for example, attention deficit hyperactive disorder (ADHD) or physical disabilities such as impaired sight or hearing. Some of these pupils may have teaching assistants assigned to them to provide extra support in class. Talking to teaching assistants (TAs) is an excellent way of learning more about specific pupils. In addition, the TA may work with the class in other lessons and may have a wealth of useful information about the whole class. You also need to be aware of any pupils that have specific problems with their health, for example asthma, diabetes or epilepsy. You need to become familiar with the subtle changes in behaviour that may occur in such individuals, for example, mood swings due to incorrect blood sugar levels in diabetic pupils, or drowsiness that could be a warning sign prior to an epileptic fit. Knowing your pupils means that you can recognise the symptoms at an early stage and act promptly to seek appropriate help.

Home–school links, though not always easy to establish or maintain, do have a significant role to play in the learning process. Most parents or carers are keen to contribute towards their child's learning and development. They can be involved in identifying and monitoring academic and behavioural targets, as well as recognising when they have been achieved. Interestingly, after speaking to parents or carers you may find that your pupils behave remarkably different at home, as this student teacher found out during a parents' evening:

> 'Sometimes you think you know a particular pupil pretty well, until you meet the parents! I was expressing my delight at a pupil that had overcome their shyness and was beginning to speak out in class. The parents asked me if I was talking about the right child. In the end I had to give a physical description of the pupil, as the parents didn't recognise that the boisterous, argumentative teenager was a little angel in school! Luckily I knew the girl pretty well otherwise it may have been somewhat embarrassing.'

Knowing how to engage your audience

Clearly, if your pupils are to play an active part in their own learning, you need to know how to engage them fully:

> '*I found that if I asked more questions, then the pupils would become more alert instead of just sitting there listening to me drone on.*'

However, questioning effectively is a skill that takes time to perfect. Directing appropriate questions to individuals means that you need to know your pupils and their capabilities.

Making the learning relevant to pupils by putting it in context and drawing on their interests and hobbies helps to motivate them, as the student below highlights:

> '*Pupils needed to connect new ideas with something they were already familiar with. It really helped them to understand and remember the ideas, particularly if the links were unusual or funny.*'

Pupils enjoy a level of independence in the classroom, and fostering a stronger sense of ownership can also signal that you trust them to take a greater responsibility for their own learning and that you recognise their growing maturity as learners.

> '*The kids loved writing stuff that they found out themselves ... set them a task to find out ten "fascinating facts" about the solar system. They liked the idea that they soon became the "experts" and were teaching me.*'

Pupils value opportunities to collaborate with their peers. Not only does it provide a sense of security, the collaboration can help pupils to express themselves and develop understanding through conversation with others. It also gives you the opportunity to see pupils working in a different context. As you circulate the room and listen in to their discussions, you can learn a lot about individual pupils; not just about their understanding of the topic, but their interpersonal skills too, for example their ability to negotiate, compromise or listen to others:

'With new classes, particularly sixth formers, it was impossible to get anyone to say anything. I ended up answering all my own questions! Getting them to discuss the question in small groups or pairs first solved the problem. At first I thought they must all be really dim, but I soon realised they lacked confidence. It took time to build a supportive atmosphere where pupils felt comfortable speaking out in front of their peers, where they knew they wouldn't feel stupid if they got something wrong.'

Making assumptions about your pupils

Observing pupils before you teach them can be very helpful, but it can also introduce misconceptions about their attitude and behaviour. There is the temptation to assume that your new class had a 'hard time' with their previous teacher and that you will do things differently. You are a reasonable human being and the pupils just need to realise this! You may feel a little uneasy about being too strict with pupils that you don't know. You may therefore decide to use a relatively liberal approach at first, to offer an 'olive branch', but this unfortunately is likely to have disastrous consequences. The expression "never smile before Christmas" does in fact have a thread of truth in it. Starting with a relaxed style can often lead to problems that are then difficult to rectify, as these trainees found to their cost:

'I knew I shouldn't be too friendly with pupils, they have enough friends of their own and don't need us as well, OK ... but still I wanted the kids to see that I was an OK kinda chap ... wanted them to like me, I guess. I wanted to give them a chance without coming down too heavy at the start. How wrong was that! I had such a tough time trying to get them back. If only I'd listened.'

Being too strict proved to be a common concern of our student teachers. Paradoxically, those teachers that have the most relaxed and friendly classrooms are those who are 'strict'. They create clear, firm behavioural boundaries within which pupils feel secure and can have fun. These teachers are not setting out to be 'liked', but they are hoping to be respected. They are respected for their good teaching and as a consequence are often 'liked'. Strict teachers have fewer confrontations and shout less, because their behavioural boundaries are understood. They are not aiming to develop a fan club; their goal is to help pupils to learn effectively, and pupils respect and like this. To do this successfully a calm, well-managed classroom is paramount. However, this takes a considerable amount of time and skill to develop.

Assumptions can be made about 'amiable' classes, as the following Science trainee described during an interview:

> 'I was observing my mentor's class the week before I took it on. Great, I thought, an easy class. The atmosphere was fantastic; all very relaxed, lots of humour, and the kids seemed to listen without being told to. My mentor sat casually on his desk and briefly explained the practical, said "off you go" and they did. Then it was my turn. All was fine during the first lesson, but things got gradually worse. I couldn't get them to listen. Practicals were all over the place and very chaotic ... they completely changed with me. It was like they were a completely different class! It was a real battle. Don't think I really got them sorted before the end of the placement, to be honest. I should have been much, much tougher from the start. I guess they were pushing me to test the boundaries? The problem was that I hadn't any, well not fixed ones, because I hadn't decided myself where they were! So they kept pushing, testing, but all they got were mixed messages with "fuzzy" edges. I didn't feel at all comfortable with this and I know they didn't either.'

What this student had not observed was the hours of training that the teacher had put in beforehand. The rules of behaviour had to be taught and learnt and continually reinforced. The boundaries have to be clear, fair and understood by all, and that includes you!

> 'I guess pupils are like puppies, they have to be trained and I hadn't done this.'

The same student was asked if things were any easier on second placement:

> 'I decided to be much more strict from the word go. First of all I thought about what my rules were, what I would accept

in terms of behaviour and what I would not. I also got to grips with the school discipline policy and I knew what the consequences were for misdemeanours and where I could go to get back up if things got serious. From the very first lesson I was a lot more formal and tried to deal with minor offences immediately. I spent the first lesson going over the lab rules and standards of behaviour. I expect it was a bit boring really, but it was worth it in the long run. I laid on the health and safety card, always a good weapon as a Science teacher! But I think what really worked for me was seeing them as individuals, not as one big mass. Somehow then they seemed a lot less scary. I learnt names as a priority so that I could home in on those messing about. Before I was a bit scared to tackle the kids, but what made matters worse was I didn't know their names, so couldn't reprimand them individually or get them to do anything much really … a disaster all round to be honest. At first I'm not sure that the kids particularly liked me, but that's where I went wrong before … wanting to be liked, I mean. I think the kids could see that they were really learning stuff … that I did really try and this included trying to be fair and consistent with punishments. Didn't always get it right, but I tried and if I messed up I apologised. Seemed to work! Mind you, I never quite got to the really relaxed, purposeful, atmosphere of my previous mentor, but I was certainly getting there. I didn't have to shout all the time and kids seemed to enjoy the lessons. I could even share a few jokes without everything getting out of control. Even had the odd thank you! Second placement gave me a real buzz, brilliant feeling. There were times on first placement when I felt like giving up, I felt totally demoralised, but now … well the PGCE is the best thing I've ever done.'

This student clearly went through a steep learning curve and made lots of mistakes along the way. The key is to work towards long-term success while learning from the short-term setbacks.

The following students realised that they shouldn't make assumptions about their pupils' appearance or implied maturity either:

'Pupils may try to act like adults and sometimes seem like they are, but they do have the minds of children. Never underestimate this.'

'The really disruptive pupils don't all look like you imagine they would!'

Conversely, don't assume that just because a class that you observe appears 'difficult' with one teacher, it will also be a struggle for you too. Classes that have a reputation for being challenging can often surprise you:

'The toughest class in the school (year 9) were, in fact, very responsive to me as a new teacher.'

This following comment illustrates the need to be flexible in your approach with pupils, as one rule doesn't work for all:

'Sticking to one piece of advice and adopting one management technique for dealing with all pupils is a recipe for disaster ... pupils are different and will behave and respond differently in different situations.'

Flexible but consistent

Although you will naturally vary your approach from individual to individual, you must be consistent with your behavioural boundaries from one day to the next. For pupils to be allowed to talk when you have asked for quiet and then be reprimanded for it the next day causes confusion and resentment. If you gave a detention to a pupil who failed to do their homework on two occasions, it would seem completely unjust to do the same for another pupil who failed to do it on only the first occasion. Pupils can accept that boundaries may vary from teacher to teacher. Though this is not ideal and schools work very hard to minimise these differences, it can be the reality. Pupils learn where their individual teachers' boundaries are, just as they learn that they need to behave differently in a church compared to a gym. Problems arise if the rulebook changes for the same situation. Pupils like to know where they are and what the rules are. Wavering boundaries cause resentment and this will affect your relationship with your class.

Knowing your pupils will enable you to administer the most effective response to a misdemeanour. You should, of course, respond to all pupils talking out of turn, but how you do this might vary. For one pupil a raised eyebrow will be enough, another may need a clear command. Similarly, some pupils prefer not to speak out in public and you may need to help them with a rehearsed response before they will do so, yet others will answer before you're part way through the question! It is important to give positive feedback to all pupils, but some detest public praise, so for these pupils a quiet word is preferable. Most of all never let anything go. Keep to your rules and reinforce your boundaries. Consistency is at the heart of good teaching:

> '*Endeavour to stick to your rules. If you vary them from lesson to lesson pupils interpret this as you being moody.*'

> '*A Physics teacher, whom I took a class from, taught me to be consistent. This meant that the pupils know what to expect and that when they did something wrong they knew the consequences.*'

> '*Invest time at the beginning, the more you chase at this stage the less you'll have to chase later.*'

Students found it difficult to be strict with a new class and with pupils that they didn't know, but realised that the clearer their expectations and the tighter their behavioural boundaries, the better. Establishing these rules from the first lesson was also identified as a priority:

> '*The best advice is to be hard; most of us couldn't imagine doing this, but it really is the only way, even if you think you're being really tough it's probably fine. Kids do respect someone who makes it perfectly clear where the line is and demonstrates what happens when it is crossed.*'

> '*The pupils really surprised me. I was so shocked at their behaviour at times that I didn't react as harshly as I should have done.*'

The power of praise

Only a few of the student teachers highlighted 'praise' in responses to prompts about classroom management issues. The power of praise seemed largely underestimated. It is easy to overlook the occasions for praise, and to react more rapidly to the need to censure. Yet positive behaviour management techniques where good behaviour is praised and thus rewarded can be very effective. The focus becomes the good behaviour rather than the bad:

> 'The positive behaviourist strategies (praise, rewards, etc.) work so effectively. The pupils that were continually seeking attention through bad behaviour began to realise that they got more of my time if the behaved!'

> 'Even able pupils won't perform without praise.'

> 'Last lesson with a year 8, I brought in a box of sweets for a treat and ended up using them all as individual rewards during a revision lesson – we got a lot done!'

> 'If pupils are lined up outside, praise the well-behaved ones on your way into the room. Check on those "messing about", but don't be too heavy-handed initially ... try humour.'

High expectations

It is easy to allow background information about your pupils to colour your expectations of them. It is important to maintain high but realistic expectations of your pupils irrespective of their home backgrounds or abilities:

> 'Pupils soon switch off when they pick up the "thick as a brick" vibe.'

> 'I was surprised that a pupil who had EAL [English as an additional language] support gained the top mark in a spelling test.'

> 'Go in with high, but not unrealistic, expectations – especially if you've been told they are a "difficult" or low-ability group.'

> 'Pupils can be turned around after support and a pep talk, especially if they know you believe in them they begin to believe in themselves.'

> 'One of my greatest successes was teaching the bottom set, and really making them work like a top set (my expectations), then eight of them gained a C Grade (Foundation) for their exam – they really surprised themselves. I was so chuffed for them.'

'One of my greatest successes was rewarding a child who had been described as a social misfit, and who was a notoriously difficult pupil. I awarded him with a bar of chocolate for being historian of the month in my class.'

Good sense of humour or class clown?

Using humour effectively is a sign that you feel comfortable on the classroom stage. Your behavioural boundaries are in place and you are not afraid to share a joke. Obviously you are not expected to be a stand-up comedian, but a little humour goes a long way. It can help to create a relaxed atmosphere, diffuse difficult situations, and chivvy awkward individuals along:

'Being a fully rounded, witty person was a great asset!'

'When pupils are lined up outside, praise the well-behaved ones on your way into the room. Check on those "messing about", but don't be too heavy-handed initially ... try humour.'

'Using a bit of humour helped to keep pupils on task – "looks like you're too busy organising your weekend to finish the questions!"'

If you say something inadvertently that makes pupils laugh, then laugh with them and don't be afraid to laugh at yourself. This will show a great strength of character and will ultimately foster respect. However, don't dwell on this comical interlude at the expense of your teaching. A brief jocular diversion works wonders, but exploitation of the comic moment may backfire; your pupils need an expert teacher not a stand-up comedian, and becoming the class clown will dent your professional image and may ultimately lose their respect for you:

'Your jokes don't have to be that funny, the kids seem to laugh anyway.'

'I was so nervous the first time I taught each class. Fear of the unknown I guess? If I could raise a smile it seemed to break the atmosphere ... well, it certainly made me feel better.'

'I'm not a very good speller and making a joke about it helped

me to cope with the embarrassment of incorrect spellings on the board.'

Laughter can sometimes be misinterpreted though, you must try not to feel threatened by it, or assume that pupils are laughing at you. Pupils often laugh when they are embarrassed, uneasy or simply don't know what else to do. Some may grin or laugh when they are being reprimanded; in this case it may be a physical manifestation of nervousness or embarrassment, as the following students illustrate:

> *'Teaching the structure of the male reproductive system to a year 7 class was a bit of a challenge, particularly with the background of giggles.'*

> *'I was telling this lad off and he sat there with a big grin on his face. It made me really cross. It was difficult to focus on the primary behaviour [the original misdemeanour] without getting sidetracked by the secondary stuff [the grin].'*

Keeping your private life private

Having made huge efforts to learn about your pupils it seems fair that they should learn something about you, but beware, you are treading on dangerous territory here. Of course they want to know about you – children and adults alike are inquisitive – but this is another route by which pupils will push your behavioural boundaries:

> *'I was surprised at how desperate the kids were to know things about me.'*

By all means share with your class the fact that you support a particular football team, or that you are a fan of a particular rock band, but it's not a good idea to discuss your latest partner, or the difficulties that you're having with your marriage, and certainly don't discuss the private lives of colleagues!

> *'There seemed to be a constant fascination in my private life: "Are you married Miss?", "Have you got a boyfriend?", "Have*

you got any kids?", "How old are you?" It was tempting to answer, but I thought if I did it would be a slippery slope and the questions would simply become more and more invasive. Some rehearsed stock replies seemed to work "Has this got anything to do with glaciation?" ... "Not appropriate" ... but the first time it happened I was a bit shocked and floundered badly!'

The relationship that you need to establish is a professional one. Once the boundaries are crossed there is no going back. It is for the sake of your relationship with the pupils that you need to keep your private life private. Your role as a teacher can only flourish if it is a clear-cut role and not hampered by sensitive information. You are neither a parent nor a friend. The relationships that you develop are special because they are set within safe limits, and maintaining that professional distance means that you can be effective as a teacher. We are only too aware of the problems that arise when family or friends try to teach us something. Being taught to drive is often best left to a driving instructor with a professional distance, rather than a member of the family! As a teacher you have a very privileged and specific role, and the pupils need you to stick to this. They need you to be their teacher, not their friend or carer.

The most important things

When student teachers were asked about the most important things that they had learnt about pupils, their responses often focussed on behaviour management issues, perhaps not surprisingly at this early stage in their careers:

> *'Make it clear that you object to their behaviour, not to them.'*

> *'Have firm not fuzzy boundaries for pupils.'*

> *'Talk to pupils outside the classroom or at the end of the lesson so that they don't "lose face".'*

> *'Be ready for students when they arrive – don't fidget and look as if you're unprepared.'*

> *'Use questioning technique as a tool for behaviour management.'*

'Wait for quiet before you speak and repeat commands a couple of times.'

'Crack down on the small things and the big things won't happen.'

'Tell them, tell them again, tell them in a different way, tell them what you told them!'

Conclusion

Getting to know your pupils and building good relationships will take time. There will be initial setbacks, but you need to think long-term because getting to know your pupils is the key to becoming a successful teacher. However, to do this and allow relationships to flourish, you need to establish a calm, well-organised, productive classroom. As a result your lessons will be more successful, pupils will feel safe and happy, and they will respect the fact that they are learning and making progress. In turn this will create the foundation for sound relationships and so reinforce the cycle:

'I think pupils liked and respected teachers in the school that were good at their job ... those that tried to do their best to help the kids to learn. I'd really like to be one of those teachers ... someone that the kids will remember ... I guess I became a teacher because I wanted to make a difference.'

Chapter 6

Learning while teaching and with teachers

Roy Barton

This chapter aims to explore the ways in which you learn how to teach whilst working alongside experienced teachers. An earlier chapter explored the ways in which the observation of more experienced staff can influence your learning. In this chapter we will look more directly at the ways in which working with your mentor and other teachers in the school can impact on your development as a teacher.

Your mentor

Clearly your mentor will have a key role to play in your preparation as a teacher, and an important element will be your working relationship with them. What can you do as a student teacher to maximise the likelihood that your relationship with your mentor will work well?

The process rests on the establishment of a professional rapport. As in any dynamic working relationship, success depends to some extent on the personalities of both your mentor and yourself, and so it is not predictable and will vary considerably from one situation to the next. Whilst you may find that you relate to some mentors more easily than you do to others, an important part of your work as a professional is to be able to establish a working relationship with all colleagues, even though it is possible that you may not find a given person particularly easy to get on with. In this context it is useful to read and reflect on some general advice from previous student teachers and their mentors.

The comments below come from a couple of students reflecting on their experiences of working with mentors:

> 'Ask for help and things you need – take the initiative – ask, ask, ask.'

> 'Say what you want or how you feel early; don't let things build up.'

These comments highlight the fact that you are undergoing a course of professional education, so you need to be an active participant in this process. However, you need to balance this advice with the knowledge that your mentor will be extremely busy with other demands on their time. It helps if specific times to meet with your mentor can be arranged and included on your weekly timetable. School life is such that it will be difficult otherwise to find opportunity for sustained or uninterrupted conversation about your progress, and you may become frustrated that you are not getting the support you feel you need. It is likely that such meetings will be a basic element of your chosen route of teacher preparation, so it should be reasonable to expect this type of dialogue.

Once your dialogue is established, it is important to respond with care. Sensitivity and tact are crucial, not only when gauging a good moment to ask something, but also in phrasing what you want to say:

> 'Take advice in a humble manner, use your own judgement about it and then act on it.'

> 'Be diplomatic and tactful.'

> 'Try to get on with all staff.'

Clearly these students were conscientious that sometimes you may not agree with the advice being offered by colleagues, and that it is not unusual for you to have to deal with conflicting advice. There is a balance to be struck between providing your viewpoint or rationale and being seen as someone who does not respond to criticism and advice. Learning to work effectively alongside a range of different colleagues is an important part of the job, as is applying sometimes contradictory guidance to your own practice and assimilating it to your own values and philosophy.

When students were asked about coping in general they made the following remarks:

> '*Always be (or appear) confident, calm, consistent, authoritative and professional.*'

> '*Stick up for yourself.*'

> '*Learn from bad experiences; don't give up.*'

> '*Maintain an open mind and be prepared to change yourself.*'

> '*Ask if you are not told you are doing OK.*'

These comments identify the importance of trying to establish a professional appearance, but recognise too that you will often feel the need for reassurance. Some of them indicate the importance of inner strength and determination, but they also indicate that you need to be continually willing to modify your approach.

As you can see, these sets of comments indicate the importance of effective interpersonal skills. To get a greater understanding on the student–mentor relationship it is useful to explore the views of mentors themselves. When asked what advice they would wish to pass onto next year's student teachers, they offered the following comments:

> '*Be open and honest in discussing problems experienced in class; don't be afraid to voice fears.*'

> '*Ask for advice as soon as problems arise.*'

> '*Always be prepared to show your teaching file to your mentor.*'

> '*Learn from lesson evaluations.*'

> '*Don't take criticisms personally – feedback is often done in a hurry!*'

> '*Most staff can only give quality time at the end of the day, so be prepared to leave late.*'

> '*Keep up a dialogue with your mentor and other staff.*'

A number of these comments allude to the tension between the mentor's assessment role and that of a supportive tutor providing encouragement. If the relationship is working well then you should feel that there is a supportive and relaxed atmosphere in which you can feel comfortable in making your first steps in the classroom. In addition to getting some things right you will also make mistakes. Mistakes, though they can be difficult to deal with in the moment, are a vital part of learning how to teach. Your mentor should make use of both your achievements and your mistakes to provide you with focused and achievable targets which will enable you to move forward. This process is called 'formative assessment', in which information from the ongoing assessment is used to identify what has been achieved and what is needed to move on to the next stage.

Guidance from your mentor

A key aspect of the mentor's role is the ability to identify realistic targets by which to structure your progress, and consequently to indicate whether your overall performance is improving in relation to these. If the process is working well, there should be no problem in your mentor moving from providing you with ongoing formative feedback to making summative judgements on your overall performance towards the end of the school placement. As indicated above, the identification of realistic and appropriate targets is at the heart of the process. If you are unclear what your next targets should be, or if you have so many identified that you are unsure which to tackle first, then you need to take the initiative and ask your mentor to clarify the situation.

Verbal feedback will form the core of the routine advice you get. A student said to me recently that it was the continuous brief verbal feedback given at the end of each lesson by all the staff involved in his preparation that was the most vital element in his progression towards meeting the standards. However, written notes on your progress also provide vital pieces of evidence on your progress towards meeting the Standards. Each course will specify its own requirements but it is in your own interests for you to take an active involvement in producing these records. One way in which routine targets can be set and progress towards meeting previous targets monitored is via a weekly written log. At the heart of this process is the acknowledgement of your progress with previous targets, as well as identifying new ones that are now appropriate and which represent a clear progression towards reaching the QtT Standards.

To illustrate this process of target setting and how it changes, it is helpful to take a snapshot of the comments provided by one PGCE student, William. Early in the first placement William's targets were related to specific tasks, for example, prepare to start a lesson with class X on Wednesday. These quickly expanded to involve teaching whole groups. It was interesting that the log indicated that William was unhappy with his first lesson but that the mentor noted that they felt the response of pupils was actually fairly typical of those occurring in the final period of the day with this year 9 class. The following week the advice moved on to discussing the need to adapt lesson plans to consider the time of day and subsequently the need for short structured tasks for this particular class.

By contrast, William's second placement logs do not have the same graded entry and are soon providing a rich mix of positive aspects together with much more detail in terms of targets. The ability to seek advice from staff and a willingness to be adaptable and flexible during lessons is picked out as a very positive feature of William's practice, echoing the advice from mentors discussed earlier. It is important to be aware that the nature of preparing to teach will involve dealing with a mixture of targets, some of which are very specific (for example, the need to summarise key points on the board) and some which are more open ended (for example, 'continue to build on the progress made with oral work'). An important indicator that William was progressing well was the way in which the targets continually moved on to describe more challenging tasks. In this case, about one month after starting the placement, William was encouraged to 'plan something different for year 10, for example project/IT work'. As his proficiency in the classroom increased, the focus of William's targets moved away from specific classroom activities to encompass other aspects of the Standards; for instance, William was asked to mark some year 10 coursework and to find out more about planning an educational trip. The target obviously encouraged greater autonomy.

Adopting different teaching styles

During your course you may well be encouraged to work in the classroom in a range of different ways, which should include the full spectrum from passive observer to solo teaching for a whole class. At first sight it may seem that solo teaching is the only way in which you will develop your teaching skills. Whilst this is a key element in your preparation, there are a number of other ways in which your teaching skills can be developed. One of these is to team-teach alongside your mentor or another experienced teacher. In principle this should provide a rich and safe environment in which to learn. There should be no worries about classroom control, and working as a team with a more experienced colleague should result in an excellent opportunity to improve your teaching skills. For example, one student suggested the experience was a way of 'observing good practice, without the pressure of having to control a class', while another indicated that it was an opportunity to 'gain experience of different ideas/techniques'.

However, as indicated above, in some cases this collaborative partnership did not work in practice:

> 'I did not like this experience too much because I was teaching with a teacher that likes being in control.'

One of the issues to emerge is the problem of sharing responsibility for a group, indicated in the following comment:

> '[Team-teaching was] ... a double-edged sword. At times I found myself relying on the teacher to lead, yet on other occasions I strove to prove that I was a capable as she was.'

> 'It was very difficult – discipline – who becomes responsible, different teaching styles. I found this more difficult than my own teaching while being observed!'

It can be very difficult for some experienced teachers to relinquish or share their classes, especially because they are ultimately accountable for pupils' learning and have no doubt formed with them complex and constructive relationships over time. This would suggest that a vital part of the approach to team-teaching is to identify prior to the lesson exactly which role each of you will adopt. One approach to assist in this process is to jointly plan the session, which should ensure that not only are you both in agreement about the objectives of the lesson but that you are clear about your relative roles at each stage during the lesson. A number of students saw this as a helpful way in which to deal with the transition to solo whole-class teaching:

'It was a good way to be introduced to the class as they got to accept me as a teacher – led to a smoother change-over when I took over.'

'At the start team-teaching ensured that my management of the class was less of an issue and I found I could get on with teaching the lesson. Authority was provided by my mentor being there around me to build up my confidence and was helpful when I took over the class on my own.'

'This was a great start as it introduced me to the pupils as a member of the teaching team, not a supply or student teacher.'

'The class gave me more credence more readily. It helped the transition to teaching solely later on.'

One of the problems of learning to teach is that you need to develop a range of skills all at the same time. In some respects this is like learning how to drive: if you were able to concentrate only on steering you could develop that skill, then move on to other aspects such as gear changing or looking out for other road users, but unfortunately you need to develop all the different skills at the same time. This is the case with solo whole-class teaching. However, with well-planned team-teaching it is possible to concentrate on particular aspects of running a lesson, leaving the rest to your mentor:

'It helped a great deal. You can concentrate on a particular aspect of teaching.'

This reinforces the comments made earlier about the benefits of jointly planning the lesson, which provides the opportunity to identify with your mentor exactly which aspect of your teaching you will concentrate on during the lesson. These are likely to reflect the current targets as discussed earlier.

However, potentially the most significant benefits come from changes to your practice as a result of working alongside an experienced teacher:

'Team-teaching a year 13 group was most enjoyable and helped with the pace of the lesson.'

> '*Being in the same room and team-teaching with an experienced teacher allowed me to view and compare styles (my own and the other teacher). It made me conscious of not imitating since doing that at the same time, in the same room, would have looked ridiculous.*'

> '*Team-teaching was a challenge but it enabled me to see how different teaching styles work in practice. It also enabled me to build up my confidence, through feedback from the teacher involved.*'

> '*Just being with an experienced teacher during lessons allows you to pick up lots of little tips.*'

> '*It helped with key questioning and how to manage a question-and-answer session effectively, keeping up pupil interest.*'

> '*Witnessing the calmness of a confident teacher – the direct affect this has on the class and on me as an "extra pair of hands" – they respond to the way you are.*'

Not having responsibility for the whole group but being actively involved in the delivery of the lesson provides the opportunity to gain an insight into the ways in which the lesson impacts on individual pupils:

> '*It often produced an interesting angle on these children's views of the lesson, if working with a group as part of the main task.*'

Team-teaching requires both the mentor and the trainee to attempt to work together. In the majority of the examples cited above, this resulted in significant gains for the student.

It may not work in all cases, but the potential gains are such that team-teaching is well worth attempting. Whatever happens, please don't complete your course making the following remark:

> '*I would have felt awkward since they were the "proper" teacher.*'

Successful team-teaching may just be a matter of finding a colleague with a style that complements your own, though that doesn't necessarily mean their approach has to be the same. Sometimes the combination of quite distinct personalities can provide a very dynamic lesson for pupils, bringing humour and variety to their learning.

Chapter 7

Learning from 'the hidden curriculum'

Marian Agombar

Preparing to become a teacher usually conjures up images of enthusing and espousing about a specific subject within the school curriculum. However, this is but a small part of being a teacher. You will be working closely with pupils in a pastoral role, being a role model for them, engaging with your own and pupils' values and attitudes to personal, spiritual, moral, social and cultural issues. You will be contributing to and upholding the ethos and values of the school and its community once you become part of that community. This chapter illustrates how student teachers come to terms with these expectations and responsibilities.

The hidden curriculum

Part of the process of becoming a teacher is thinking not only about your own classroom and your own subject, but also about the whole school community of which you are to become a part. 'Professional Values and Practice' is one area of the QtT standards (TTA, 2003) which contains phrases such as 'communicate sensitively with parents and carers, respecting the social, cultural, linguistic, religious and ethnic backgrounds of pupils, treating pupils consistently and with respect and fairness, and particularly that they [i.e. the student teachers] demonstrate and promote the positive values attitudes and behaviour that they expect from their pupils' (2003: 1.3) and that they can 'contribute to and share responsibly in, the corporate life of schools' (2003: 1.5).

As with anything called 'the hidden curriculum', this area of the role of the teacher can be quite difficult to define: if it's hidden, how do I know I am dealing with it? You may ask! And how important is it, if it is not in the 'open'? *The National Curriculum* (DfEE, 2000) talks about the values, aims and purposes that underpin the curriculum. It states that as well as thinking about a productive economy, education, both at home and school, is seen as 'a route to the spiritual, moral, social, cultural, physical and mental development, and the well-being of the individual', so that 'education should reflect the enduring values that contribute to these ends. These include valuing ourselves, our families and other relationships, the wider groups to which we belong, the diversity in our society and the environment in which we live. Education should also reaffirm our commitment to the virtues of truth, justice, honesty, trust and a sense of duty' (2000: 10). This then becomes the second aim of the school curriculum: 'to promote pupils' spiritual, moral, social, and cultural development and prepare all pupils for the opportunities, responsibilities, and experiences of adult life.' Further explanation of this includes phrases such as passing on 'enduring values', developing 'pupils integrity and autonomy', enabling pupils to 'challenge discrimination and stereotyping', promoting pupils' self-esteem and emotional well-being, helping them to 'form and maintain worthwhile and satisfying relationships, based on respect for themselves and for others' and developing their ability 'to relate to others and work for the common good.'

These sound like rather ambitious targets, and not easily quantifiable, or perhaps even discernable in the work of the school or the teacher. However, there are areas in which teachers do work for these aims, largely in the pastoral side of their role, which is one that few can actually ignore. During the PGCE course at the University of East Anglia, a number of student teachers choose to investigate a whole-school issue which brings them into direct contact with this aspect of their role, and it may not be something which they had actually expected to become involved with at all. Reflection on the implications of this for their future professional development often indicates that it can change their perspective of their role in schools.

This chapter will look at some of the learning that has taken place according to a selection of these assignments, and the answers to a questionnaire given to students at the end of their training, and some reflections on these by a few. The questionnaire asked student teachers to reflect, as they completed their training, on:

- whether there had been aspects of the teachers' role that they had not expected;
- if they had been involved as a form tutor during their school experience, and whether this had been an enjoyable part of the job and why;
- whether they had been involved in PSHE and how they had felt about this;
- their position as a role model for pupils;
- the effects of being involved in extra curricular activities with pupils; and
- how they managed to get on with particularly difficult pupils.

At interview and in their personal statement on application, potential teachers talk about their love for their subject and their desire to share this enthusiasm with young people. While we do expect applicants to have some idea of what this might entail in the school context, it is often only putting it into practice that brings an awareness of the wider scope of the teachers' and the school's role. The assignments and the questionnaire look specifically at areas which go beyond teaching and learning in the classroom and move into more personal areas. Reactions to expectations in schools, which are seen as part of being a good colleague and a good teacher by the pupils, often depends not only on the subject knowledge and teaching skill in the classroom but also in the approach a person takes to the other persons on a human level. It is often difficult to disentangle the good teacher from the reasonable human being, but we are intending to look here at student teachers' reactions to their part in enabling pupils to become reasonable adult human beings in due course.

> 'I had not expected to be so keen on ensuring that pupils are OK. My concern for their well-being has been entirely unexpected, and my worry when they are not OK has at times disturbed me, as I thought I would be able to forget about them on walking out of the school gates. I want to deal well with the pastoral side of the job, and feel this as important as my subject teaching, if not more so.'

This was the reaction from someone who had just completed the PGCE course, and shows how the process of becoming a teacher had meant an unexpected interest in the pupils themselves:

'Showing children how to be a good person: what behaviour is acceptable and what is not. Now I believe that this is the most important aspect of teaching.'

These sort of comments raise questions about what a teacher is actually doing – is it teaching a subject, meeting targets and assessment criteria? Or is it something deeper and perhaps more subtle than this? Something which, when you start the process of becoming a teacher, you may not have expected, but becomes increasingly important in your mind as you enter into your role and the life of a school more fully. Certainly many at the start of their preparation to teach do talk about their love for their subject and their enthusiasm to share this with young people, and it is certainly important. But you may begin to wonder whether it is your subject or your enthusiasm that is the more significant, and you may reflect on why you decided to become a teacher yourself – was it the subject which engaged you? Or a teacher of that subject who inspired you? And how do you feel about the pupils that you are about to teach? Our first voice talked about actually worrying about pupils and taking that concern beyond the school gates. The second began to think of the teacher as being a role model, and that behaviour is more than only the behaviour management issues in the classroom, and moves into being a 'good' person. Another comment also echoed that:

'As teachers we need to set a good example and educate kids outside of our subject matter – drugs, morals, social behaviour, in order to prepare them for adult life, not just exams.'

This takes the role of the teacher more specifically into areas which go beyond the remit of many of the more usual 'subjects' as timetabled and into areas that are now often covered within the Personal, Social and Health Education frameworks, and may well be part of time spent with a tutor group. It also acknowledges that the purpose of education is bigger than gaining paper qualifications – adult life needs more than these, but an ability to cope with many issues and decisions do not gain a GCSE grade.

It is this area that is often referred to as 'the hidden curriculum', and is described in some documents and the criteria used in the inspection process, as the spiritual, moral social and cultural development of pupils which needs to be attended to in schools. This runs through all the subjects and the other aspects of school life. It is concerned with the whole area of 'ethos' or 'values' in the school. It may not be part of the formal curriculum but has something more fundamental about it – about the way the school community treats and values the individuals it contains, and how such values are transmitted. They may not be formally taught at all, but they underpin everything that happens, from dealing with unacceptable behaviour to pupils with particular learning needs: from the decisions about school uniform to meetings with parents and carers. As a teacher you will be expected to take your part in all these 'hidden' aspects of the way young people are educated, and you may find, like our two student teachers, that this is an aspect of your role that you find of particular interest or importance to you.

A teacher is said to be in loco parentis, and this must also mean that there is a duty of care – a certain responsibility to think about the well-being of the pupils in the school and not see them only as potential GCSE grades or numbers in an A-level class. This is often known as the pastoral side of the teacher's role. One of the student teachers noted that they had not expected to need to be a 'parent/listener/shoulder to cry on' although on reflection this had seemed natural when faced with the pupil's need, as did one who said:

> '*Although I expected involvement in pupils problems to some extent, I was not prepared for dealing with the grief of one of my form who lost his brother just before his GCSEs.*'

Of course not everyone will meet this specific situation, and certainly not in their training year, but when we are dealing with people it is always uncertain just what will be required.

The role model

What it means to be a role model needs to be considered carefully as you go into schools for the first time as a teacher. How do you handle pupils' interest in you as a person? How much information are you prepared to share with them? How do you set the boundary between your desire to be a friend as well as a teacher? This can be particularly difficult for a younger teacher who seems to be more of an older sibling than an authority figure/role model.

> *'There were several occasions where pupils would try to engage me in conversation about my personal life, and I often found myself having to bite my tongue and avoid sharing details with them.'*

It is an easy trap to fall into; although it feels as if you are creating good relationships, pupils do not always have the same view. It is a fine line between being friendly and being over-familiar. You may wonder also if pupils are really interested, or are actually trying to trap you in some way, so that the need to 'bite your tongue' is felt even more keenly. There are also occasions when the pupils will ask questions to ascertain whether you have the vices you are counselling them against:

> *'Miss – do you smoke?'*

> *'Sir – did you get drunk?'*

How do you answer that question, being both honest and yet acting as a role model? The student teacher who became aware of the need to be a role model when 'they found out that I smoked' did not elaborate on the effect this had. It is difficult to be credible to pupils if you follow the 'do as I say, not do as I do' type of advice; for example, if you have told the pupils off about mobile phones in the classroom, you become acutely aware of your own position as a role model:

> *'When my mobile phone went off in class!'*

When pupils find an excuse to 'hassle' you they are inclined to make the most of it:

> *'I have a tummy-button ring which some year 7s noticed when I was putting up a display. They asked to see it and I said no, but they hassled me – I didn't really know what to do or say.'*

And some discussions can be quite difficult. Do you tell pupils your own opinion, admit to it if you are asked, or do as this student teacher did:

> 'We had a debate about tattoos and personal choice and I happen to have a tattoo which I kept very quiet!'

Of course the location of the tattoo may have influenced this person! Sometimes avoiding the whole issue is the easiest way to tackle it, but this is not always possible.

While these examples may appear somewhat trivial, they can provide moments of stress, embarrassment and do confront you with the questions about your place as a role model for adolescents. Other examples cited show how these lesser issues can lead the way to meeting more difficult problems. The following student teacher felt that a rapport had been developed which led to a position of trust as part of their duty as a role model:

> 'When it came to light that a serious sexual incident had occurred to one of my pupils, they trusted me and I was responsible for dealing with it and passing it on to the child protection officer.'

And there is almost a note of satisfaction that such trust had been earned.

On the following occasion the student teacher is modelling an appropriate reaction and giving the message about the values of respect and tolerance that a school is promoting:

> 'There were incidents of shocking name-calling where I had to really tell pupils off – hopefully my reaction would inform pupils' opinions.'

And this instance also suggests that the student teacher became aware of the need to be a role model when reacting to emergencies and individual pupils:

> 'Handling of medical issues – showing you are calm and controlled in front of the class. Your response with pupils with problems and issues, how you deal with pupils on subjects other than what you are teaching them.'

Some of the student teachers were obviously given a great deal of respect and trust when pupils sought them out for help.

> *'A year 11 pupil from my form group came to ask me about how to deal with the stress she was under. Given the demands of the PGCE, I felt able to give her advise and to understand what she needed me to say to her.'*

> *'A victim of bullying came to me for counselling and it became obvious that she had no positive male role models in her life.'*

Here, as well as offering advice, the student teacher became aware of a real social need which some pupils have for good role models in school to compensate for a deficit in their family and social life. It is impossible to include this kind of demand made on teachers in general in a training manual. It tends to be through actually dealing with the problems and taking advice from experienced teachers that you do learn to provide an effective role model, in occasions such as countering 'racist comments in class, sexual comments, breaking up a fight.'

'When some year 8 girls developed a crush' was identified by one of our student teachers as a result of being seen as a role model. The need to handle this type of situation in such a way as to reduce embarrassment for all sides is something only practice can really equip you for, although advice is available from those who are supporting you in school.

Being a form tutor

The most obvious time when teachers meet the pastoral side of their role is as a form tutor, and you will be given some experience of this during your time in schools. Those whose experience is limited often sound regretful about this. Six student teachers were negative about their role as a form tutor, preferring to meet pupils in the teaching rather than in a pastoral setting. Two others were ambivalent, saying that they had enjoyed it 'in terms of pupil relationships' but not ' in terms of excessive paperwork and report writing'. One of the negatives said 'I found it very difficult to differentiate between a "teacher me" and a "form tutor me". I prefer to teach than tutor.' This suggests that the two 'personae' of the teacher here are different, and may be an area that you need to think carefully about. Not all teachers enjoy this aspect of the role, and you are not under an obligation to do so, though many teachers find this side of their work rewarding. Within the sample surveyed most of the remainder, that is, another 40 student teachers, expressed their enjoyment of this side of their experience in schools. It is an opportunity for you to meet pupils on a different footing and discover more about them, and while some mentioned that there are the demands of paperwork and administrative tasks as well, these appeared to be outweighed by the relationships with pupils:

> '*I loved being a form tutor. I though it was a very valuable experience which I thoroughly enjoyed. I can't wait to get a form of my own. It's great to see another side of the pupils.*'

> '*I really enjoyed my time as form tutor. I developed a strong bond with the class, something I shall always remember.*'

> '*I found it very rewarding – it was a bit of a shock at first being thrown in at the deep end with a year 11 group, but it was nice to be able to support them through their revision periods of crisis!*'

The use of the word 'rewarding' here is an interesting one. What are the rewards of being a teacher? It seems from this that it is being able to actually make some sort of difference in the pupils' lives – for the better – and is one of the intrinsically satisfying parts of being a teacher. From a sense of alarm at the expectation to an awareness of actually making that difference – 'supporting' them as a moment of 'crisis' – is the reward.

The opportunity to see children away from your own speciality subject area allows you to have a different perspective on them. You are able to see them as people in this setting more than you can perhaps in lesson time, where their attitude and abilities in relation to your subject tend to be foremost. Outside the lesson they may be able to compensate for any shortcomings in it.

> '*It was enjoyable to see the children in a different context, to find out what they were like as people and to see that even if they weren't great at my subject, they had a thousand other strengths and interests.*'

'It allowed me to assess pupil behaviour outside my own lessons. It also gave me an insight of how behaviour is influenced throughout the day.'

It may, however, make different demands on a teacher, as the person who felt that this was not their strength has already stated, and as this student teacher noted:

'(You) get to know the pupils on more of a personal emotional level. I felt like a different type/sort of teacher, which was nice.'

This may cause you to ask what other sort of teacher there might be.

And it does bring its own challenges. It may be during this time that a teacher is asked the more personal questions which were mentioned previously. If you have the opportunity to get to know your pupils better, they also have the same opportunity with you.

'It is a different and closer relationship with pupils, although it is difficult to strike a balance between the approachable and yet remain professional – especially with younger pupils.'

It may also be the same for you as this student teacher, who said that the form group was 'the only group I had time to really get to know' due to the way the timetable is arranged or allocated to your subject.

'I like the fact that I always start the day with the same pupils and am able to develop relationships with them in a non-teaching context.'

Here you can see that it can offer you as well as the pupils a sense of routine that is almost independent of the varied daily timetable, and also away from the concerns of the subject, which can be a welcome change:

'[It] gave me the chance to build up relationships with pupils outside of the curriculum subjects and deal with problems other than Geography-related ones.'

Personal Social and Health Education (PSHE)

You may also find yourself being asked to teach about areas outside your own subject as part of the PSHE curriculum, which is concerned with the wider areas of pupils' development and brings in more explicitly the area of attitudes and values. This aspect is now part of the compulsory curriculum, but schools may implement it in different ways. This may be in form tutor groups rather than with a timetabled lesson or in some other cross-curricular way. So, for example, as part of PSHE historians found themselves teaching about exploitation with examples of prostitution and incest, a geographer taught drugs and sex education, a scientist taught about the problems of bullying, and a modern language specialist about dental hygiene! Some enjoyed it and found it worthwhile, but others felt it was beyond their competence at this stage. How much assistance you actually receive to put this into practice will vary. You will at some stage have to decide your own reaction to this aspect of the teacher's role.

'It's OK if teachers feel comfortable with the subject' said one of the student teachers, acknowledging that this is another area where teachers have preferences and may also lack some expertise.

'I didn't think it was useful and would prefer it to be taught by specialists' said another student teacher, which again suggests the need for some expertise in this field. It might be that this person felt unable to make a useful contribution rather than PSHE itself is not a useful area for schools to cover, although another said that they believed PSHE covered 'some material that is the parents' responsibility'. If we link that to a previous comment about the lack of some role models, it may cause some thought about how far the teacher has to act in loco parentis in developing the values and attitudes of the young people who attend schools.

Out of school activities

You may well have opportunities to be involved in a variety of extra-curricular activities during your school experience. Such events are part of a school's ethos and demonstrate the value that schools put on the wider education of the pupils. Our student teachers thought that such involvement had had a very positive effect on their relationships with the pupils and consequently the classroom became a more pleasant place to be in, and therefore possibly a more effective learning environment. To some it demonstrated that the profession they had entered was a complex one, perhaps more than they thought. Joining in the Duke of Edinburgh award scheme showed one mathematician that there is 'more to teaching than just in the classroom', and this links back to the comments at the beginning of this chapter about what being a teacher is actually about. It was not an unexpected side of teaching to this person, but rather a way to learn more about the role itself.

Joining in school trips and other activities:

> '*broadened my knowledge of those pupils I was dealing with. They were more friendly and I noticed they treated me perhaps with a bit more respect.*'

> '*It was really rewarding to see these kids out of the school context and made me aware of their backgrounds and interests.*'

This student teacher took part in an 'Activities week – initiative test, rounders, roller skating. You get to see pupils in a different light, and vice versa. They respect you more for joining in and having a go, even if you do make a fool of yourself.'

These comments indicate that this is a two-way process for both teacher and pupil, and can involve a certain amount of risk, which is often present in the forming of relationships. As well as the teacher knowing more about the pupil, the pupils also learn more about the teacher, which is again seen in a positive light and has the potential to make a difference in the classroom:

> '*I played football, which gave a chance to be known as a person, not just the RE bloke.*'

And they recognise that there is a genuine interest in the pupils here too:

> '*You interact with pupils as an individual where any agenda you may have only concerns their well-being, not learning objectives.*'

> '*I took part in the school's production of* Oliver, *which allowed bonds to be formed, and some pupils viewed me consequently as "more human".*'

This comment makes you wonder how pupils view teachers who are not prepared to join in other activities – are they less human?

The impossible pupil

It is also necessary to be aware that it is not always possible to form good relationships with some pupils, and coming to terms with this type of rejection can be painful. You will learn a variety of strategies to cope in these circumstances, including using help from more experienced staff members and senior staff too, so that you can remain within a school's policies.

One particular student teacher was prepared to share this story, which shows the need to think very carefully about the area of relationships, and not always to take the whole responsibility for them perhaps, even if you do feel that you should be the one 'in control':

> *'I had a year 10 pupil in a mixed-ability group. I took the class over from a female teacher in her thirties. I observed the group and immediately noticed one pupil. Constantly talking shouting out answers, he had a comment about everything. Their current teacher said afterwards, "Oh, you'll learn his name first!"*
>
> *It all started reasonably. I learnt in the first few lessons that if instead of constantly battling against the chatter, he responded better if I let him answer a few questions early on and then the rest of the lesson was easier. I moved him away from his buddy who usually egged him on. On a one-to-one basis I worked hard at building positive working relationships with pupils. I started to gain respect. However, this particular lad seemed to respond very negatively.*
>
> *At first it was small-scale, for example, passing comments as he passed in the corridor, often just a look or a seemingly innocent comment said in a malicious or derogatory tone. I think that's what made it so tricky. There was nothing really I could report. It all seemed such small-scale and unnecessarily petty events. But there were lots and it made me feel very uncomfortable, as a woman confronted by a man and as a human being disrespected by another, not just a teacher undermined by a pupil. I felt I should be far more in control. He was only 15 and I was the teacher. I learnt his background had led to little appreciation*

for authority or females in general. I knew things like this could affect whole careers and to be honest I was really afraid. It got worse and began to encroach on lesson time. A song in the charts at the time referred to a young female teacher and a male pupil's attitude to her in a sexual reference; he began to hum it in class. How could I report that he had hummed a song – that to me did not seem like an issue that I could take to the senior management.

I think that took me the most development; to realise that it was affecting me as an individual, his education and personal issues as well as the attitude and teaching I was providing for the whole class. That meant it was something I definitely had to pursue. I had no support at this stage; as a new teacher in the first few weeks of my career I was unaware of what I should do or what options were available to me. I know now that instead of sitting in scared silence I would confront or even recognise this situation much earlier on. I would also know now what to do about it.

It all came to a head when he made blatant comments such as "Have you got a younger sister, Miss; if she's six months she's too old" or "Where are you taking me on Friday, Miss, somewhere quiet I hope". I went to my link tutor, cried my eyes out and tried to express how unhappy it had made me. I referred it to his head of year and he was removed from my classes for the last week.

I learnt a lot about how easy it is to ignore petty troubles and allow them to build up. I also feel sympathy for the lad who is going to confront more troubles without realising where it stems from.'

You will not necessarily confront this kind of difficulty, but it does show how important it is, as a new teacher, to seek help, and do so at an early stage. It was certainly a learning experience for the student teacher concerned, and she was later able to see it as such, despite the distress it caused at the time. On reflection she was also able to see that it was the pupil who was in more serious difficulty than the teacher, and that he would have more problems to deal with in his life. You may find a school which actually has counselling for troubled pupils and may be able to help in this kind of situation. Similar stories can be found from male teachers who are the subject of a 'crush' from the girls in the school, which can also become very difficult to handle.

Other student teacher comments indicate that many did have to put up with behaviour which they found difficult to cope with, but senior staff and mentors did support when asked. Some of them, though, had a feeling of failure when help had to be called on. One piece of advice that may help is that all teachers, however long they teach, find some pupils very trying! And of course we cannot make friends with everyone, but we do have to find ways to work with them. This may be through our own attitude:

> 'There was one girl that decided that she absolutely didn't like me. First of all I made it clear that her behaviour was unacceptable. I also made a real effort to be nice to her and say hello in the corridor. I made an effort to smile when I saw her. This made things bearable. I tried to get to know her even though she was not very forthcoming.'

> 'I came to realise that you can't reach every child or have a positive relationship with every pupil, you just have to try!'

Or through a real attempt to engage them in their learning:

> 'One pupil in particular generally did not want to be in school. I discussed strategies for engaging his interest with the Head of Department, Head of House and Form Tutor to enable me to personalise his learning.'

Or use of the behaviour system and other members of staff:

> 'Some very immature year 7 boys in one class would try and wind me up but I successfully squashed them – just didn't let up, saw/spoke to them individually and once one of them had visited the Head of Department they realised I wasn't going to put up with it.'

Alternatively:

> 'I think it's important to try and find something nice about even the naughtiest of kids. Try to find out what they are interested

in outside the school and take an interest in this; they'll like you more for trying.'

'I moved him as far from me as possible to stop him irritating me, but I also went to basketball training where I knew he would beat me to let him see my human side.'

These last two comments show how meeting pupils on different ground is also recognised as helping with problems in the classroom.

A final comment, or rather a piece of advice, from another student teacher:

'Don't take it personally: take advantage of any support you are given.'

Other issues

Some student teachers have issues that raise questions about the area of values before they start their training. For the group we were talking to these revolved around how to deal with sensitive issues in the classroom and disclosures of a sensitive nature from pupils, and they were asked later how they had come to terms with these. One student teacher talked about deciding that if you were aware of potential sensitive issues that should be enough. To teach whilst always trying to avoid them was like 'walking on eggshells' and made life very difficult. It was better to treat the pupils who may have problems normally, as to do anything else could actually make the situation worse through over-compensating.

A History student teacher was concerned about some areas of his subject which could be difficult in the classroom, such as the Holocaust, the slave trade and Islam. At the end of the course he had come to accept that sensitivity and professionalism could solve the problem. 'I was also a little surprised by the fact that ignorance and prejudice were not "colour bound", with pupils from different ethnic backgrounds often engaging in racist behaviour. Perhaps this was a prejudice of mine that needed addressing.' Certainly being aware of our own bias on such issues is important if we are to give a balanced picture to the pupils. He went on to say, 'On reflection I actually found the most sensitive issues the most rewarding to teach, despite them providing different challenges to "safe" areas of study.' This may lead us again to think about the real purpose of education, and whether by being prepared to address some of these difficult issues pupils are actually gaining more in terms of attitudes and skills, rather than simply knowledge. Perhaps too, when faced with controversial issues, teachers take more care with lesson preparation and with the way the lesson develops because of the 'risk'.

Another area that concerned those entering teaching was the possibility of pupils telling them things which were related to their well-being or safety. Already we have noted occasions when they were called on to offer advice on stress, and to counsel victims of bullying. This was something raised by one student teacher at the initial stage, and at the end of the course she wrote:

> *'My experience in my two placement schools has helped me to develop strategies for responding to pupil disclosures. Through seeing other staff dealing with issues and through direct experience on my placement I have learned appropriate responses to pupil problems. One particular experience with a 6th form pupil who was being verbally abused by another girl enabled me to learn how to inform the appropriate people and to discuss the issue sensitively with the pupil concerned. A great deal of handling pupil disclosures is informed by common sense, intuitive pastoral skills and an awareness of the correct school procedure regarding specific issues.'*

The very personal and specific nature of each incident does make it very difficult to meet all the needs that you will find in school during any course. Learning though experience is very important, and the nature of the many preparation courses is intended to offer the opportunity for this and support that experience for student teachers. Pupils do come to school with a variety of problems which are not related to school but do have an impact on their ability to learn. If the school can provide a suitably supportive environment some of these can be solved or at least alleviated.

Other areas that relate to this idea of the school ethos or values in 'the hidden curriculum' concern the use of school uniform, pupil motivation in school, looking at the incidence of unauthorised absence, using single- or mixed-sex groupings for teaching, television violence and its possible affect on pupils' behaviour, and behaviour and eating habits, and many more. The school's response to such matters as school uniform or bullying or unauthorised absence indicates the values that the school seeks to promote. One student teacher concluded that all the school staff need to be supporting the shared values of the school if the community was to tackle effectively some of the problems which pupils' behaviour presents, either in terms of discipline or in attitudes to school.

Having surveyed attitudes to school uniform, one said:

'I have been able to see the issue from the pupils' perspective and analyse how different their viewpoints are compared with those of adults. The important point for me to take away is that pupils are free-thinking individuals whose rights must be protected, with or without school uniform.'

This student was then able to recommend that:

'it may be in the school's best interest to have a school uniform policy provided they listen to the pupils and try to meet them half way on a uniform that is both practical and comfortable for the pupil.'

The school (or at least the adults in charge) believed that having a uniform would contribute to the prevention of bullying. Our student teacher decided that 'there is no magical solution to stopping school bullying and improving discipline. Much of this answer lies in the chemistry that exists in the school between the pupils and the staff ... the pupils themselves make the ultimate decision on behavioural change.'

Looking at the issue of single-sex or mixed-gender classes led another to see that:

'School should be a place where we teach cooperation and attempt to bring down the barriers between the sexes. If we teach pupils from an early age that they cannot interact on the same agreed level, what hope have we of creating a society where all people have equal opportunity to achieve their full potential ... By doing this investigation it has made me look at my own stereotyping within the classroom ... Our behaviour as teachers and educators can be the deciding factor as to how our pupils achieve, behave and develop. For my future teaching I will try and incorporate tasks that appeal to pupils of both sex and attempt to look at them as just pupils rather than male

or female pupils. I will try not to let my own expectations affect the way I handle situations in the future.'

What started out as something specific about the organisation of a classroom for teaching purposes had made this person realise how the messages being given to pupils in the way we as teachers approach problems are as significant, if not more so, in their education as the content of any lesson. It also revealed to them some prejudices and preconceptions which had to be challenged in order to make this person a more effective teacher.

And that the classroom is only one part of a whole was also suggested to this person in another study:

> *'My study of the sanctions and rewards system at the school has given me a greater appreciation of the link between my classroom and the whole school. In retrospect I feel that during my first practice I tended to use sanctions in terms of what I felt appropriate for what was happening in my own classroom without sufficient regard for what the school was trying to achieve as a whole. In future I will make sure that I am aware of school sanction policies so that my classroom practice supports endeavours to improve cross-school behaviour.'*

If the school is to work effectively it does need everyone who works in it to be following the same set of values which underpin all the work that they are trying to do with the pupils. As a student teacher in any school you will need to find out how these are expressed in a variety of ways and become aware of the part that you play in the transmission of the values and attitudes to the young people in your classroom, your form tutor group or those clubs, activities and expeditions you take part in with them. You may have mixed feelings about the pupils themselves, but hopefully you will feel like the student teacher who said about her form group:

> *'The little scumbags were adorable.'*

Chapter 8

Learning to work within frameworks

Terry Haydn

Teaching offers opportunities for professional autonomy yet at the same time is bound by a number of constraining frameworks and requirements which monitor what is taught, learned and assessed. As a student teacher you will need to learn how to cope with the requirements of the Standards in Qualifying to Teach, the National Curriculum requirements, GCSE and A-level examination syllabuses in your subject, as well as the organisation and management of the school and department you are working in. This chapter reflects on the challenges to student teachers as they strive to fit in with the professional and social frameworks of becoming a teacher.

The importance of understanding and working within frameworks

Every year, thousands of people decide to go into teaching. Most of them are motivated to go into teaching at least in part because they feel they can do it well, can 'make a difference', have a beneficial influence on the lives of the pupils in their care, rather than primarily for financial gain or because teachers get long holidays (Kyriacou and Coulthard, 2000; Spear *et al.*, 2000; Hutchings *et al.*, 2002; Cockburn and Haydn, 2004).

And yet, as anyone who has been to school as a pupil knows, not all of them develop into inspirational and outstanding teachers. Some work for several decades in classrooms and never rise beyond anodyne and mediocre levels of competence. Others quickly become very accomplished and effective classroom practitioners, even within the period of their initial training.

What are the characteristics of those teachers who fall into the latter group? When you start your course of initial training, has everyone got the same chance of developing to excellence or are some people more likely to succeed than others, by virtue of their innate abilities or previous experience (a couple of years in the SAS, psychiatric social work, stand-up comedian)?

One of the paradoxes of life as a teacher is that over the medium- and long-term, it is a job that offers a large degree of professional autonomy, scope for originality and creativity, the chance to develop your own 'style' of teaching, and your own approaches to particular topics. And yet during your period of initial training, you are obliged to work within a variety of frameworks, your work is closely monitored, and you are a long way from being a 'free agent', able to teach whatever you want, in whatever way appeals.

Media representations of teachers and teaching often portray the profession as ideal for 'off the wall' mavericks and individualists (the film *Dead Poets Society* is one that springs to mind). In the first week of our course, we spend a great deal of time and effort trying to convince our students to realise that they are not free agents, and that probably a primary objective in the early stages of the course is that they understand the importance of 'fitting in' and developing an understanding of the various frameworks which circumscribe their professional lives.

The most obvious of these are the standards for the award of qualified teacher status (DfES, 2002), which outline the competences that student teachers are obliged to attain before they can be unleashed on generations of children. The standards are explicit in noting that 'only those trainee teachers who have met all of the standards will be awarded QTS' (TTA, 2003: inside cover).

Although the QtT standards are clearly central to your progress over the course of your training, there are several other frameworks which, it could be argued, are equally important. You are not a free agent, a 'freelance' teacher; teaching is essentially a collaborative activity. You will be teaching within a department, which will have its own schemes of work, its protocols for homework, planning and assessment, its principles and priorities. You will be part of a school that has its own ethos, its systems for managing pupil behaviour and its systems of communication. You also have to work within curriculum specifications such as the National Curriculum for your subject, and you have to develop a knowledge and understanding of a range of government strategies for improving teaching and learning. Whether you are a student on a PGCE course, a SCITT or a GTP programme, you will also be part of a taught course, which will have its regulations, guidelines and expectations. You will also be operating within the constraints of what I will argue is an overarching framework of particular importance, even though it is in some respects an unwritten one; that of teachers' expectations of colleagues in terms of their overall professional attitude and approach.

You should keep in mind the existence of these frameworks because many commentators (see, for instance, Stenhouse, 1975; Klemp, 1977; Elliott, 1991) have argued that it is the quality of teachers' understanding of these frameworks, and their ability to operate intelligently within them, that is the principal determinant of how successful they will be in their work. There is more to teaching than a series of technical teaching competences ('Can use a whiteboard', 'Can use PowerPoint' and so on); part of becoming an 'expert' teacher is your understanding of the contexts you work in, your 'situational understanding' (Elliott, 1991: 128) of pupils, classrooms, staffrooms and colleagues.

In probably more than several of the other chapters in this book, I have drawn on the testimony of experienced mentors and curriculum tutors as well as that of student teachers. I believe that triangulation of these perspectives demonstrates that it is possible to discern some of the key characteristics of working successfully within frameworks, which are the hallmark of effective (and therefore fulfilled and successful) teachers.

Working with the 02/02 standards for QTS

In 1998, Anthea Millett, Chief Executive of the (then) Teacher Training Agency, argued that by spelling out more comprehensively than ever before the competences which trainee teachers would be obliged to possess before being licensed to teach, the standards for the award of QTS would ensure that the breadth of newly qualified teachers' competence would be higher than ever before (Millett, 1998). To add further rigour to the process, and further ratchet-up standards, the Teacher Training Agency announced the introduction of online 'Basic Skills Tests' in literacy, numeracy and ICT, which all trainees would have to pass before QTS could be granted. This competence-based approach has to some extent replaced the more traditional emphasis on student teachers acquiring a knowledge and understanding of 'the four disciplines' of education (Philosophy, Psychology, Sociology and History of Education) which previously characterised teacher education in the UK (see, for example, Aldrich, 2002).

In effect, the standards are a list of things that you must be able to do/to know in order to qualify to teach. One of the potential advantages of spelling out an extensive range of competences is that it obliges student teachers to consider the range and breadth of factors that are involved in becoming a fully effective, accomplished teacher – to realise what a complex and difficult job teaching is. Several students commented that focusing their classroom observation of lessons on a particular strand of the standards was a good way of making lesson observation more purposeful and of getting acquainted with them.

Against this, student teachers can feel overwhelmed when confronted with such an extensive list at the start of their training. Which ones have to be approached first, in your first few weeks of teaching? Another possible problem with the standards as they are set out is that there is no indication that some standards may be more important than others. Also, there is no explicit acknowledgement that in many areas it is not just a question of whether you are able to 'tick-off' the competence, but your level of competence that will determine your effectiveness as a teacher. Your ability to interest and motivate pupils (standard 3.3.3) might range from 'occasionally achieves this, and at a fairly modest level', to 'is often able to inspire and enthuse pupils' (extracts from mentor reports).

So how do student teachers deal with the problems, dilemmas and choices that arise out of the 02/02 standards? The following extracts from interviews, reports, evaluations from student teachers, mentors and curriculum tutors, attempt to provide some insights into how to approach the challenge of working with the 02/02 standards. The comments include advice from student teachers to the next year's cohort, gathered at the end of the PGCE year.

Many student teachers reported feeling overwhelmed by the breadth of the 02/02 standards when they considered them in the early stages of the course:

> 'You're feeling fairly nervous anyway at the thought of having to go into a classroom within the next few days, and to stand

up and teach in front of real, live pupils at some point. In the first week I just felt overwhelmed with information ... Not just the standards, but the forms, the course handbook, the subject handbook ... It was only when I had my first meeting with my mentor that I felt reassured ... She made it seem less daunting by not waving the standards in front of me and persuading me that they were a sort of ... further down the line thing ... The early stages of first placement were more about just getting familiar with the feel of being in a classroom and learning how to talk to pupils appropriately, to act normally and try to relax and be yourself.'

'My mentor on first placement told me that as long as I demonstrated that I was conscientious and dependable, worked hard to prepare my lessons, showed that I wanted to do things well, listened to advice and acted professionally with pupils and colleagues, that he would pass me. It wasn't that he ignored the standards ... he just made it clear that they were a long-term agenda ... you didn't have to address all of them in the first few weeks.'

When asked about in what ways they used the standards with student teachers, several mentors pointed to a major difference in approach between first and second placement.

On first placement:

'I try to get them to think about what you need to get by ... to survive ... to look at the standards and think about what they must be able to do to get through the day ... They've got to be able to teach from the front of the class ... to think hard about things like exposition and questioning ... how to talk to pupils in an appropriate manner ... what to do if kids start to mess around ... devising a range of activities which will get them through the lesson ... and if at all possible, to try and find ... do something some of the time which will hopefully get the pupils interested and enjoying the lessons.'

'We go through the standards and think about which ones are first placement ones and which one might leave until later. They have got to learn that there is more to it than keeping them occupied and getting them to behave, but it's understandable that in the early stages this is what preoccupies them ... At

least if they can do this they get chance to think about some of the "second order" things – what about the quiet kids in the corner, what about the kids who are really bright and are not being stretched.'

'If at the end of first placement they can plan and teach a lesson, they have got some idea about how you talk to pupils, they've got on well with colleagues and been generally conscientious and dependable and shown a willingness to listen to and act on advice, that's the main thing ... that's the platform which makes you think they can go on to become good teachers.'

On second placement:

'It's their responsibility to look at the standards and think ... what next ... what haven't I thought about yet ... what should I think about or try out this week? I can suggest things, point to where they might direct their attention and energy, but certainly towards the second half of second placement, they should be beginning to take responsibility for their professional development ... that's what they will have to do in their NQT year.'

'You have to adopt a much more systematic approach to the standards. We make a conscious attempt to think methodically about the different areas of the standards. This involves coming back to particularly important bits like class management, planning and assessment. I probably wouldn't do things like CATs, PANDAs, YELIS etc. [assessment instruments] on first placement, but it's important that they know what these things are by the end of the course.'

'I want them to understand what "plateauing" means ... and to understand that there is more to it than just getting them "on task" and quiet ... that this doesn't necessarily mean that they are learning anything. Good trainees have got a real sense of initiative in relation to the standards ... they get on with it without having to be prompted but they also keep talking and discussing what it means to be better as a teacher.'

Student teachers' comments also showed a change in attitude to the standards as the course progressed:

'Not a list to be ticked off but helpful to think about what next, or what to try and make progress in next week ... Some things more urgent or important than others ... you've got to look at them in relation to how you are doing and what sort of school you are in, what your classes are like. Just self-analysis was as important as anything in not plateauing ... Having time at the end of lessons to think it through. And the talk with your mentor at the end of the week ... thinking more broadly or strategically rather than just thinking ... that lesson went OK.'

Part of the skill of surviving and doing well on the course was felt to be the intelligence and insight with which students approached the standards. Keeping them in perspective, thinking about priorities in the context of their teaching placement, realising that there were perhaps some 'core' competences that were particularly central to effective teaching, that some competences were more important than others, and that you needed good judgement and guidance to work out which to address straightaway, and which might be left until later on the course. These are some comments from curriculum tutors in response to a question about which students seemed to make best use of the standards:

'The ones who keep them in perspective ... who can almost put them to one side and not worry about them in the first few weeks or work out which are essential for the "survival" stage, but who really focus on them once they are established and who keep them in mind week by week, especially when on the long second placement ... so they just get better and better in understanding all the things that good teachers are thinking about when they teach. Even in the last couple of weeks of the course, they are still looking for things which they might not have really thought about.'

'Students who realise that it's not just a matter of ticking off a strand of the standards, but of thinking how good they are in it on a continuum between hopeless and brilliant ... particularly in areas like exposition and questioning, which they will use in nearly every lesson ... and how skillfully they talk to pupils, which is another really key skill for teachers.'

'I don't want them thinking about their ability to use ICT if they are really struggling with planning or class management.

It's the intelligence with which they prioritise the standards ... This is often helped by the quality of the professional dialogue which they establish with colleagues ... whether they can act on advice and are genuinely open to learning.'

'It's interesting to look at evaluations ... some genuinely "attack" a strand of the standards ... they really work hard at grappling with it. With others, it's just good intentions ... it's cosmetic ... "Must do something about this group next lesson", "Must not talk over them" – written but then not acted on. No follow-up comment on how it went in the next lesson. You can read through the evaluations and they have not made any mention of three-quarters of the things that are in the standards.'

'Some of them genuinely engage with the standards, they think about them, they talk about them with colleagues, but they realise that they need to think about other things as well – it's not just about ticking off competences, there are other ways of looking at what's involved in being a good teacher – reading about "My best teacher", reading about other perspectives on progression as a teacher.'

The point about responsiveness and being open to learning was also made by an experienced mentor:

'Some of them get things even before you have mentioned it to them... they seem to have really good intuition about how things have gone and what they need to think about... some you mention something to once and they grasp it and start working on it. Others you have to tell them more than once... some just don't really take things on board... they just carry on as before.'

One of the most common problems that we encounter with our students is that even towards the end of their training, they have failed to consider the full breadth of the standards. You are obliged to keep a teaching file which contains a record of your planning and evaluation of lessons, and to gather evidence that you have fulfilled the competences stipulated in the 02/02 standards, and this is subject to the scrutiny of your mentor, your curriculum tutor, and possibly external examiners and Ofsted inspectors. We are aware that many students (understandably) find the business of writing learning objectives and lesson evaluations tedious and time consuming. It is, however, one of the most important sources of evidence about your progress in the 02/02 standards, and nearly all the curriculum tutors and mentors I have spoken to regard it as one of the most reliable indicators of the student's level of capability – it is unusual to encounter a strong student teacher who has a chaotic and inadequate teaching file, and vice versa.

One suggestion which some students said they found helpful was to rephrase the statements in the 02/02 standards as questions which they might be asked at interview; for example, 'Do you feel that you know how to use ICT effectively to teach your subject and to support your wider professional role?'.

The standards are not perfect, and they are not the only framework you have to think about in preparing to be a teacher, but if you use them intelligently, they can play a big part in helping you to become an effective and successful teacher, by helping you to avoid 'plateauing' in your learning, reminding you of the breadth of things there are to think about, and in helping you to realise what a complex and difficult job teaching is.

Working with curriculum specifications and government strategy materials

Acquiring a grasp of the National Curriculum for your subject, the external examination specifications, and the government 'strategy' materials which have been developed in recent years are all part of the development of your understanding of your subject (see sections 2.1 to 2.7 of the 02/02 standards; see also Chapter 3). As with the standards for QTS, the quantity of information which students are confronted with at the start of the course in these areas can seem overwhelming. Several students felt that it was important to stress that you have to take a medium- to long-term approach to assimilating all this information, to accept that you can't get to grips with it all in one go in the first few weeks of the course.

> 'This stuff all comes on top of the anxiety about the classroom management side of things, which is quite high-profile in people's concerns at the start of the course. You need someone to tell you that it's alright not to know everything straightaway. Some people get really worried just before the start of first placement.

The first priority should be to prepare for the classes you are going to teach. Becoming reasonably confident on the topics you are teaching and knowing the basics of the National Curriculum for your subject are probably the most urgent priorities.'

'It took me over a term to become really familiar with all facets of the National Curriculum for my subject and the examination syllabuses in my placement school. The sessions we had on the Foundation Subjects Strategy were helpful and gave you some ideas, but there was too much to take in at one time. It's a question of accretion, of gradually becoming familiar with the various bits and pieces you have to cope with.'

'Don't let the strategies [numeracy] rule your life. They are useful guidance but don't have to be your bible.'

'Your heart sinks when you see the thickness of the folders, but if someone takes you through it or tells you about bits, there are generally some good ideas in there somewhere which do speed up the rate at which you develop good ideas to improve your teaching.'

'It speeds up the rate at which you make the transition from thinking about what you are going to do, and thinking about the pupils and what they are learning.'

Curriculum tutors talked of the need for students to pick out the parts of strategy documents which they found helpful and relevant, rather than attempting to digest them whole.

'On one hand, these frameworks can be helpful, but they're not the sole genesis of ideas for effective teaching.'

'There are some problems when they start with the literacy strategy as a base, not trusting their own judgement. They should use ideas from the strategy documents "off the peg", having confidence in their own subject knowledge, adapting ideas in the light of what works for them.'

'They need to read the strategy documents critically ... There is sometimes not an easy match between the National Curriculum and the Literacy Strategy objectives – it can be difficult for them to see the links and relative status of the two frameworks.'

'I am often surprised at how few of them have looked at the values, aims and purposes of the National Curriculum (section 2.2 of the 02/02 standards) so that they can think about in what ways their subject might contribute to these. Often the strongest students are the ones who find time to read in order to develop their pedagogic subject knowledge, that is to say, how to teach the subject in a way that makes sense to pupils ... being aware of the full breadth of ways in which pupils might benefit from studying the subject.'

Becoming aware that there is more to subject knowledge than substantive content knowledge (just 'knowing your stuff') is an important part of becoming an effective teacher, but this is not a short-term agenda. It takes years not months to develop to 'expert' levels in all facets of subject knowledge (look at the breadth of section 2 of the 02/02 standards if you doubt this), but this does not mean that you do not have to address these agendas, you just have to do it gradually, as the course progresses. By the end of the course, you should have at least made a start in all of these areas, and be working to develop your knowledge further.

You also need to read strategy documents critically. Teaching is not like bricklaying or plumbing or playing a technically correct backhand drop shot on the squash court, where there is generally a 'right way' to do it. There is rarely any technique which can be guaranteed to work for all pupils, in all classes, in every school. As Stenhouse (1975) argued, the purpose of educational reading and research (or what might be termed 'ideas' about teaching) is to provide teachers with ideas that they can test out against their own experience. Becoming familiar with the curriculum specifications for your subject should provide a clear understanding of what you are supposed to be trying to achieve in teaching your subject to pupils. Perusal of the materials emanating from the various 'strategy' initiatives should provide you with some ideas for how to achieve those objectives, although it is important to remember that they are only one source amongst many. You also develop your ideas about teaching and learning by reading relevant books and newspaper and journal articles which are not part of the government's strategies. This again demonstrates the complexity and difficulty of learning to teach. You have not got time to read everything, so there are difficult judgement calls to make in terms of what you read and how quickly you attempt to cover the 'official' documentation relevant to your subject.

Working within the framework of the department

I think that the first target we set for our students is that after their first two-day visit to their placement school, they ensure that the department they will be working in is left thinking that they are going to be a pleasure to work with.

It is difficult to overstate the importance of 'fitting in' to the departments and schools in which you will be doing your teaching. It is as important to be a good colleague as it is to be a good teacher. What I want as much as anything at the end of my students' teaching placement is that the department will be very sorry to see them go, and wish that a job had been available in the department so that they could have continued to work with them. In discussions at mentor meetings and in talking to heads of department, it is often acknowledged that from the point of view of the head of department, what they want as much as anything when making a new appointment is 'someone they can work with', someone who will get on with colleagues. This is often seen as just as important as (but not a substitute for) technical ability as a classroom teacher.

This is not a matter of fawning sycophancy and supine and unquestioning compliance with departmental ways of working and styles of teaching. It is to some extent a question of how sensitively and intelligently the student teacher 'reads' the department, and how quickly and adroitly he or she understands the values and attitudes of the department, what they think is important and what they see themselves trying to do as a department. Students who are successful in quickly settling in to working in the department tend to be observant, good listeners, and have excellent interpersonal skills. They use their intelligence to understand the 'culture' of the department. There is a tact and diplomacy agenda; it would be unusual for there to be no points of difference between beliefs, value systems and working practices of the student and members of the department. It is a question of timing and the manner in which student teachers discuss issues of professional judgement with the colleagues they work with day to day. Even if you don't agree with advice given, the sage nod and attentive demeanour are more appropriate than rebuttal and counter-argument, certainly in the early stages of the placement. Keeping an open mind and being prepared to try things out and act on advice (even if you are not sure it is the right way forward) is important. These are some comments from curriculum tutors on the attributes of students who are more and less successful at skillfully integrating themselves into the life and work of the department:

> '*I have had some students who have been very comfortable on their placement, who are looking for a carbon copy on second and because the school is different, the department is different, they are working with different people, immediately put it down as not as good ... a sort of deficit model ... It's important to go in with an open mind and be able to simply step back, wait and see. The first couple of days are very difficult for any student ... operating in a different context, it wrong-foots many students ... who are put off by it and it takes them a while ... The best of students tend to keep their powder dry for a while, so to speak, wait for a while ... it settles down ... usually, even some who are initially unhappy come round to the school and get used to the differences and see it as part of the challenge.*'

> '*Weaker students tend to make very rapid, concrete and firm verdicts on the department, the mentor, the school or very limited evidence ... This can lead to a downward spiral ... the school picks that up ... it can quickly lead to mutual tensions. I sometimes have to go out and try to get them to give each other another chance. More accomplished students seem to grasp very quickly that it is in the nature of schools and departments to differ and that this is part of the test.*'

> '*X noticed a huge difference between his placement schools but he has thrived in both. He is sincere about his teaching but not over-earnest ... he keeps a sense of perspective and a sense of humour about the differences and quietly get on with it.*'

> '*You can learn from bad practice as well as good. Obviously I like it when the student and the department are very happy with each other, but part of learning to teach is how to handle things when they are less than perfect and you have do the best you can in the circumstances.*'

> *'They are best when they are prepared to work within "grey areas". Some cope better than others in zones of uncertainty – they learn to work things out for themselves and see it as a chance to develop a sense of professional autonomy, whilst realising that they have to work within departmental guidelines and policies. They need to be flexible about the way they do things.'*

Advice from students on handling this framework 'intelligently' confirms the existence of an 'etiquette' of fitting in to a department:

> *'You can see some students saying too much too soon in the staffroom, being a bit too forward or assertive in their opinions, trying too hard. Being a good listener, taking things in, showing an interest, asking a few but not too many pertinent questions … you gradually get used to the feel of the department … whether they take the piss out of each other or whether they are quite "straight" and fairly formal.'*

> *'Try to make sure you are well organised or at least give the appearance … Try to appear enthusiastic and interested … make it clear that you are listening to advice and trying to act on it … in the same way that you show the driving instructor that you are looking in the mirror when you take your test.'*

> *'Take all advice with a pinch of salt. You will be bombarded with stories, ideas, gripes etc. Some are great, some will just make you cynical. Try and acknowledge both sorts graciously … it is usually sincere and well intended, even when it's off the wall.'*

> *'Make yourself aware of school and departmental policies. Makes it a lot easier when you know what is the departmental norm for things or "the school way" of doing things.'*

Compared to areas such as understanding how pupils learn, 'fitting in' to a department is comparatively straightforward, and some might say it was almost a matter of common sense, of demonstrating 'reasonable human being' qualities such as politeness, consideration, helpfulness and dependability. It is generally made easier by the fact that most teachers possess strong 'reasonable human being' qualities, enjoy working with student teachers and see it as an interesting and important bit of their jobs. But every year, in spite of the inordinate amount of time that we spend emphasising the importance of these qualities, in the first week of the course, before the students' first visit to their placement school, we receive several phone calls from schools saying that they are very concerned about some aspect of the student's behaviour after their first two days in the department. It appears to be more about self-awareness and interpersonal skills than academic ability and intellect.

Working within the framework of the taught course

Curriculum tutors emphasise that some of the same precepts apply to your demeanour on the taught course as when you go into school to become part of the department:

> 'Student teachers sometimes make the same mistakes that pupils make in schools. Students who are in some ways very intelligent can be opinionated . . . dominate discussions . . . very firm views . . . often rather forceful . . . not picking up the vibes in the room . . . one of the skills of a teacher . . . get the antennae out . . . look at body language . . . Being a bit quiet at first, taking your time is not a problem.'

Curriculum tutors value students who have an ability to listen to the views of others, who are sensitive to the feelings of other members of the group, and who have a sense of when they might have said enough and need to let others into the discussion or debate. They enjoy working with students who are willing to share ideas and experiences and who will be supportive of others, share experiences and mistakes, be genuinely open-minded about different ideas about teaching and learning rather than dogmatic and closed about ideas about teaching. One curriculum tutor deliberately changed the composition of working groups in teaching sessions so that over the course of the PGCE year, students would at some point have to work with every other member of the group. At the end of the last session, he asked the students to reflect on the characteristics that made some people particularly enjoyable and helpful to work with. Given that in interviews for first teaching posts, heads of department often cite 'someone who I feel I can work with and who will get on with other members of the department' as one of the most influential factors in deciding who to take on, developing insight into these 'interpersonal' attributes and agendas is a useful learning experience for student teachers.

All the tutors who were interviewed felt that it was important that students understood the status of the taught course; that it was a course of professional training and that students who missed sessions or who were frequently late elicited real warning bells and would quickly be considered a 'cause for concern'. Other 'alarm bells' included the inability to meet deadlines, lack of tact and politeness, inability to work constructively within group activities and coming to sessions unprepared.

It is important not to forget that part of your quality of life when you are preparing to be a teacher is the quality of your interaction with your peers who are also going through the process of learning to teach, and the degree to which you benefit from their experiences, ideas, encouragement and support. One curriculum tutor pointed out that 'some students are much more alert to the benefits to be derived from listening to and learning from their fellow students'. Student teachers interviewed at the end of the course particularly emphasised the benefits to morale and psychological well-being which social contact with fellow students could provide, and strongly advised their successors to keep in touch whilst on school placement, even if it was just by phone call and email rather than going to the pub on Friday night to compare details of pupil atrocities and other low points:

> 'Keep in touch with your curriculum group over the first few weeks of placement. Their experiences and encouragement is invaluable and seems to make you realise you are not alone.'

> 'Keep in touch with other students when you're on placement. They'll understand what you are going through better than anyone else. Sometimes it helps just to know that others have had a really bad week and are finding it difficult.'

> 'It is important not to just look at documentation, textbooks … on your own … Time to think … Part of what helped me to get better was the time I spent thinking about things whilst walking the dog on the beach, or talking it through on the phone with friends in other schools or by email.'

> 'It's also to be honest about making mistakes and sharing

those with friends ... you learn from each other and learn to recognise things that are a problem for lots of you ... Having people to bounce ideas off. It's no good just sitting at home brooding about things in a corrosive sort of way.'

It is important not to underestimate the weight attached to your overall performance on the taught course. You are not just being assessed when someone is at the back of the classroom taking notes on your teaching performance; everything you do says something about you, and teachers will be making tacit judgements about many facets of your presence, actions and persona while you are working with them in schools.

The most important framework of all?
Teachers' codes of professionalism

It was interesting to note that when we asked mentors to give us feedback about mistakes that student teachers commonly made, which could be passed on to the next cohort, over three-quarters of the comments related to the students' overall professional attitude and approach rather than to aspects of technical competence in teaching. Some examples are:

'Do mark books up to date at the end of your placement?'

'It's very difficult to accept criticism, even when it is offered in a positive way, but it is an essential ingredient of the mentor's task to give advice/criticism, and it needs to be accepted in a graceful way.'

'Not turning up for duties.'

'Reading fiction/magazines/newspapers in the staffroom.'

'Suggesting that the school's curriculum/department schemes of work be changed on the first day in school.'

'Don't think the school day always ends with the bell.'

'Don't expect colleagues to clear up after you – make sure you leave teaching rooms tidy.'

'Don't yawn/fall asleep during observations – even if it's boring.'

'Make the effort to be proactive, offer to help and do things, but not in a way that is too pushy. Even if the offer is turned down it creates a good impression.'

'Try not to arrive just before school begins and rushing off immediately the last lesson ends.'

'Try to plan ahead and give notice to colleagues when you need help/resources etc.'

'Don't leave school without asking your mentor, carefully check school and departmental expectations about being in school.'

'Don't chew gum in lessons that you are observing.'

'Always return school and departmental materials promptly at end of placement.'

'Don't miss registration/form period etc. to do last-minute photocopying.'

'Don't ask to cut short a mentor session, if it's booked, to catch early bus etc.'

'Always let the school/department know if you won't be in or if you'll be late. Err on the safe side in terms of dress code.'

'Not getting involved with students during lesson observations.'

'Don't say too much too soon in the staffroom.'

Whatever 'official' frameworks are laid down, there is an unspoken code of conduct constructed by the general body of people who are teachers. Part of this is about self-interest. Because teachers generally have to cover colleagues who are absent and therefore lose a precious non-contact period, they do not like 'two days a fortnight' merchants who are often not in school because of minor or non-specified ailments. But part of the code is not about self-interest; on the whole, teachers are quite a 'moral' group of people. Paul Grant, Head of Robert Clack School, questioned the tabloid portrayal of a cosy conspiracy of teachers colluding in low standards and mediocre performance: 'It is not in their interest; a peer group of professional colleagues does not welcome into its ranks incompetent teachers. Colleagues have very low tolerance levels for such teachers, and on the very rare occasions when such teachers appear, they [the staff] demand that action is taken' (quoted in Haydn, 2001: 427).

So when judgements are made about your suitability to enter the profession, whatever the standards for QTS say, teachers also think about some overarching questions which go beyond specific teaching competences. Would I want this person teaching my kids? Would they be a good person to have in the department? Are they trying to do the best for the pupils in their care? Would they be a good colleague? What will they be like when no one is watching? How will they cope when things are not OK – there are sometimes occasions in teaching where things are not as they should be but you still have to make the best of a bad job and just get on with it. Part of it is how people cope with adversity, it is about having the will and determination to become a good teacher no matter what obstacles stand in the way.

Conclusions

Teachers do have to learn to work within frameworks. One of the determinants of how good teachers will become is how intelligently and diligently they have engaged with the standards for QTS, with the curriculum framework for their subject and with the professional and social frameworks which they encounter during the course of their training.

It's not just a question of how quickly you acquire baseline competences, but about 'trajectory'; how good a teacher will you become in the longer term; how quickly do you learn, how well do you handle 'conscious incompetence'? Klemp (1977) argued that developing professional competence was not just a matter of application and intelligence but 'cognitive initiative', defined by Elliott as 'the way performers define themselves as actors in a situation. It is related to whether they see themselves as capable of changing a situation rather than as helpless victims of events' (1991: 129).

As one student remarked:

> 'At first I was angry and felt that tutors were not telling me things that would be helpful to know and which would make my life easier. Then I settled into teaching and began to learn. Eventually I realised that you have to work things out for yourself; to work out your own questions and find your own answers to them.'

As well as intelligence and determination, student teachers must also possess self-awareness. Of all the 02/02 standards for QTS, perhaps the most important is section S 1.7:

> They are able to improve their own teaching, by evaluating it, learning from the effective practice of others and from evidence. They are motivated and able to take increasing responsibility for their own professional development. (DfES, 2002: 7)

How good you will become in the longer term, the extent to which you will develop towards excellence, depends also on your determination to work to the highest possible professional standards, the realisation that part of the pleasure of being a teacher is getting better at it and doing it really well. As one of our students remarked (perhaps with a degree of irony) in an end-of-course evaluation, 'Perfection is our aim; excellence will be tolerated.'

Chapter 9

Learning about yourself

John Gordon

This chapter explores what it feels like to learn to teach, how it affects how you perceive yourself and how others think of you. The comments you will find here come from the responses of over sixty student teachers to two simple prompts, explained in the main text. The students were representative of a range of subject specialisms including Mathematics, MFL, Science, History, Geography, Physical Education, Religious Studies and English.

I try to always be myself: I have no one else to be

'I try to always be myself: I have no one else to be' is the response offered by one student teacher to this deceptively simple question: To what degree do you think you are 'yourself' when you teach? It's also a conundrum, because it indicates what might at first appear self-explanatory – that we can be no one other than who we are – while also complicating matters by saying that we might try to be ourselves, as if 'yourself' might not be a given or natural state, but rather something to be sought and realised through conscious and deliberate effort.

It is also a response that contradicts the somewhat ragged hypothesis that influenced the original question. The question derives from a hunch of mine, partly drawn from working with student teachers over a couple of years and partly drawn from receding memories of my own experiences of learning to teach. Behind the question lies a vague, fairly instinctive feeling that learning to teach might involve drawing on aspects of your personality that you didn't know existed; that it might even involve inventing a new 'teacher self', possibly numerous teaching personalities. If any of these things do happen, perhaps they don't happen easily. The first suggests that surprises – pleasant or otherwise – are part of the process, while the latter implies effort and reflection. One author researching teacher education has coined the term 'emotional work' (Evans, 2002) to describe the challenge of coming to terms with teaching, of working out yourself as a teacher. It may be a useful idea here, if teaching is to some degree about the emotional business of considering yourself in relation to situations and other people. You will find as you read that remarks which at first appear straightforward can actually be loaded with implication: that attempting to express what it feels like to learn to teach is 'emotional work' in itself, where an expression may not provide a clear sense of 'what it feels like' but can convey the curious and intriguing weirdness of becoming a teacher.

The responses student teachers give to this single question are diverse. You will find that there is no consensus, though you might find as you read their comments that patterns do emerge. For me, they make clear that the experience of learning to teach can be very different from one person to the next, and that in this sense at least it is important to be aware of yourself and your reactions during the process of becoming a teacher. If your own experiences match those described here, you may find you have no choice but to reflect. Pupils, classes, particular situations – all can make you self-aware in the necessity of a moment.

For some, the process of learning to teach seems to involve passing through a stage of discomfort, even anxiety, where 'being yourself' is difficult. It is as if the ability to feel 'natural' in the classroom depends on all sorts of other factors – a whole array of decisions and actions which eventually set up a situation that allows you to feel comfortable. This could be true for teachers at all levels of the profession, not just to student teachers, but the early stages of teacher preparation involve some additional issues, such as the attitude classes might have to a student teacher, the fact that you probably don't have your own classroom, or the influence of your mentor. One student remarked:

> *'I think particularly at the start, it is very difficult to be yourself*

in the classroom. So much is happening that you need to be aware of: what you are saying, how you are acting, what the pupils are doing, what the class teacher/mentor is writing on their observation sheets. I felt that at first you were expected to imitate their mannerisms and style of teaching. As your confidence grows, though, it becomes easier, you relax, you know the pupils and teachers more and so as the weeks go by it becomes easier to be yourself and let your personality into the classroom.'

It's a helpful summary of some of the things you're likely to think about as you begin to learn to teach, and a foreshadowing of some of the other feelings you'll find expressed here.

Acting up

A number of responses find and challenge an assumption latent in the initial question: that teaching offers even the slightest possibility of being yourself. One student teacher comments:

'I do not believe I am myself when I teach. I have become a good actor,'

while another remarks that she is 'not at all' herself once inside a classroom. Instead, she finds she is 'more loud, confident', more 'energetic' than the person she considers herself to be beyond it. She also suggests that different teaching situations demand different styles of acting, drawing a distinction between her behaviour when working with individual pupils and when teaching whole classes. Some responses are yet more specific, offering a rationale for 'acting' decisions made while teaching. These student teachers feel that there are times when they are pretty much 'themselves', but also that something about different classes and specific pupils leads them into what they feel is an act, something other than their natural behaviour:

'It depends upon the class – with some classes with a more mature attitude I could be myself, have a joke and still maintain discipline and a suitable learning environment. Other groups were incapable or unwilling to know "when to draw the line",

> *therefore it was very difficult to be myself – they made me much harsher than I would like to be.'*

Suggested in this example is the idea that it is easier to be your 'normal' adult self with classes that recognise and keep within whatever boundaries have been established by the 'usual' teacher and perhaps the school. When this student teacher indicates that the classes less willing to 'draw the line' prompt from him different behaviour, he touches on an impression held by almost one-fifth of the students involved in the survey. When he says 'they made me much harsher than I would like to be', we find a hint that one of the most difficult aspects of learning to teach involves coming to terms with the responsibility for 'maintain[ing] discipline and a suitable learning environment'. It's hard for many to take on that authoritarian role.

A similar response to the 'disciplinarian' aspects of the teacher role is suggested in this example:

> *'To an extent teaching is acting. I am flamboyant naturally and don't like being strict, so I have to put on "anger" and shouting at pupils.'*

There is aversion and discomfort here – 'I *don't like* being strict' – and a suggestion of compulsion – 'I *have to* put on "anger" and shouting' – as if teaching demands something of you that's not part of yourself. The use of inverted commas around 'anger' is interesting too. Used with 'puts on', it appears that this student teacher wants to place a distance between his 'naturally' outgoing self and the discomforting use in his teaching of this act, this necessarily artificial approximation of an emotion. It's possible that as you learn to teach you may even become aware of this discomfort at the moment of reprimanding a pupil, as was the case for this student teacher:

> *'The only time that I am not really myself is when I have to tell a child off . . . I didn't want to start giggling . . . it's just not me . . .'*

Maybe there is something odd and difficult about taking on responsibility, about being an authority figure within an institution. We may wish to place the behaviour required at a remove from the person we are happy to accept as our normal self, a self we like to think of as being in a state of serene, placid equilibrium.

Could it be that for some of us it is necessary to 'act' as a defence mechanism, a coping strategy in a strange situation? Some student teachers liken what happens when they teach to putting on a disguise, affecting a new personality. One student describes learning to 'exaggerate or mask certain traits'; another of coming to 'understand the masks' she has to wear. Sometimes the mask is worn as a reflex-action, involuntarily, and presented negatively in relation to the person the student teacher considers to be their 'true' or 'normal' self:

> 'I certainly don't feel I'm entirely myself when I teach. I am not as relaxed and don't find myself using the same sort of humour ...'

For others, wearing a mask is presented more positively, part of a gradual process of transformation:

> 'I feel I have "become" a teacher. I took a while to develop this persona, but during the second placement I felt I finally was ...'

In this example, the student teacher indicates that she has shaped and crafted her teaching persona, her own mask. She suggests an intention, successfully fulfilled: a process of working towards whatever mental image she holds of who an ideal teacher might be. Another transformation is apparent in the comments of this student:

> 'Generally I am quite quiet and introverted, yet in front of a class I am more extrovert and outgoing.'

This time the transformation seems to occur not so much over a period of weeks or months, but over the threshold of the classroom: when 'me' becomes 'teaching me'.

Mr Nasty actor-type thing

Again and again responses to that first simple question start to talk in terms of deliberateness, intention and strategy. Many student teachers indicate that they very deliberately create or manipulate a persona in the classroom, often in response to the nature of the class they teach:

> *'I tried not to be myself at all. At the start or before a lesson I would try to psyche myself up and get into character – this would vary a little depending on the class. I would feel too vulnerable to offer "myself" to a class.'*

> *'I do put on an act because I have to be sensible, authoritative and stick to the rules. Normally I'm a very laid-back person, but I have to pick pupils up for everything being a teacher.'*

> *'At the beginning of placement you try and be very strict, later you can relax more. I think your character always shines through and you can't be completely different. You can use acting as a tool, sometimes positive, sometimes negative – but not throughout every lesson.'*

Perhaps there is a link between the vulnerability felt by one student teacher, and the suggestion of another that they need to act in order to be 'authoritative'? It seems as if very positive qualities may have to be suppressed or controlled in order to create a relationship with pupils that also promotes a good atmosphere for work. The second remark hints that different situations draw on different aspects of personality, while the third makes a distinction between 'positive' uses of acting and 'negative'. Would 'positive' uses involve the teacher taking on the role of a character as part of an explanation or activity? Are 'negative' uses those that make us think 'I am not really like this', for instance if we find ourselves raising our voice to reprimand a pupil? If both uses are necessary to shaping an appropriate context for learning, it may be better to view both personae as positive, both as necessary.

As you learn to teach, then, you may find yourself adopting masks strategically. Early on this may be for reasons of personal comfort – getting to grips with being this funny thing called a teacher. You may feel very conscious of how your classes perceive you, only feeling comfortable as 'yourself' when pupils present no challenge to your authority as teacher. One student teacher feels she can be herself 'only with groups I have in the palm of my hand', another that:

> *'It varies between the classes that I teach. With some classes if*

they respect me and do what I tell them to, you can be yourself and more relaxed – this can only enhance your relationship with them.'

Some appear to see the 'act' as part of a process of becoming familiar with a group:

'At the start I tended not to be "myself", but as I get to know the pupils better, I relax more and become myself.'

'I can only be myself with the class once my authority has been established, then I can start to relax. If I do this too early then the class will not know how to respond without getting carried away ...'

While this student teacher's remarks suggest the act is conscious, the result of choosing a persona to fit a class and a situation could be varied:

'I think it depends. With some groups I was completely natural with them. However, with some it was a complete Mr Nasty actor-type thing. I think it depended on the situation.'

In this sense the act is used strategically. It is something other than 'just being yourself' or 'acting' – there's more to it than those simple opposites, and the choices you make may be influenced by your own age and gender.

In these examples, it seems that some student teachers feel more 'themselves' with pupils of a particular age:

'I find with the younger year groups I have to cultivate my strictness more. I am more relaxed with the GCSE and A-level classes. But overall I feel I can be myself and am comfortable in the classroom – which has been a pleasant surprise. I find it tremendously rewarding talking to the pupils about their ideas, and discussing them.'

'You have to be yourself as much as possible. It is easier to be yourself with more mature groups, but at the same time you can have a lot of fun with year 7 and year 8 pupils.'

Could it be that with pupils aged around 11 and 12, there

is a need to adopt an overtly adult persona? Maybe the young student teachers offering these comments find these pupils less self-disciplined, or find themselves in a position where they become far more aware of their own age relative to that of their pupils. Maybe they identify with or at least remember adolescence more keenly, but find it a challenge to establish who they should be in relation to these more obviously young, 'childish' secondary pupils.

It seems that some classes, just by being what they are, can prompt us to be more conscious of ourselves as teachers and how we are perceived. They call for us to take on different personae. In the examples here, more 'childish' classes and groups that challenge boundaries cause us to be more self-aware, can lead us into what feels like more mannered behaviour. But is it more mannered, or is it just that these situations are examples of relative extremes, and as such they pull us up sharp? Maybe we act with other classes too, but the behaviours we fall into there are less discomforting, less 'otherly' – parts of ourselves we are happier to call and recognise as our own?

Hyperself?

For every student teacher who talks about classroom teaching as acting, there's another who believes it is impossible to be anything other than 'yourself'. These responses describe teaching as though it brings to the fore an exaggerated version of yourself, an essential part of you; if you like, your 'hyperself'. Where comments provide such an account, they often describe 'becoming more settled and relaxed'; a point when teaching becomes more second nature, more 'automatic'. It's worth emphasising the 'second' in 'second nature' here. An early phase of discomforts and anxieties is passed through to reach a stage of 'naturalness', as reiterated here:

> 'I think it is impossible to not be yourself when teaching – some part of your personality will always come across to the young people. However, as I become more settled and relaxed with classes I find myself being more and more expressive and also more willing to take risks, for example being more light-hearted and 'loosening the reins' a little. I also try to bring some of my background and interests into the lessons I teach.'

The phrase 'I find myself' indicates a self-awareness, an effort that echoes the phrase 'I try always to be myself'. Maybe the 'self' that is found once you become more relaxed with classes is not really a 'true' or 'natural' self at all, but a state in which you are no longer self-conscious from one moment to the next about yourself as teacher. It's 'second nature' in the sense that it is not your non-teaching self; 'second' in that it's an alternative to that version of you, 'natural' only in so far as it becomes more comfortable. To return to the term offered at the start of this chapter, it involves less 'emotional work' and so impinges less on your consciousness.

Some student teachers appear to have a sense that as a second nature this nature can be made, constructed by them. To pick up on points made earlier, it can be used and shaped deliberately, strategically. This student responds to a common teaching cliché that seems to warn against being too light-hearted too early on:

> 'They always say "Don't smile until Christmas" and stuff like that, but I believe you have to be yourself and really let your personality shine through. A sense of humour is also very important, and confidence is also a key factor as well as the need to be consistent in your behaviour management.'

This student seems to be very clear about what allows her to establish appropriate working conditions: confidence and consistency. Presumably using humour (an attribute of her non-teaching self?) does not create difficulties because it is used cautiously, consistently, with intent. Notice that this student teacher mentions 'behaviour management', which suggests something other than dealing with overtly poor or unwanted behaviour. Unlike earlier comments on pupil behaviour in relation to 'yourself', this student has a sense that pupil behaviour is not just reacted to or against, but shaped and influenced by her own behaviour. 'Behaviour management' is a term large enough to include the way she manages her own behaviour, as well as the behaviour of her pupils. For this student humour – though associated with what she regards as her true, possibly obscured but potentially 'shining' personality – comes to be used as a technique, out of an awareness of how and when it is apt to use it. Is this so different from acting? This quite conscious manipulation of personal attributes comes across in other responses too:

> '*I teach and talk as I do normally – without the swearing. My humour is also transplanted into the lesson. I don't put any false demeanour on.*'

There's a distancing from acting here, but deliberate self-censorship. 'Transplanted' is an interesting word in this context too – isn't that rather considered, meticulous, designed?

There are also some responses that make the previously suggested polarisation of acting and being your self seem like a red-herring; that actually the two positions fit together without contradiction:

> '*I think aspects of your personality are more exaggerated in front of a class because you are putting on an "act" to a large degree. However, I don't think you can avoid your true personality coming through . . .*'

> '*In many respects I think I am "more" myself when I teach. In order to convey approval/disapproval I am happier, more angry, more elated when something positive happens. I think that teaching often (though not always) involves a degree of acting. From observation of colleagues I have found the least effective teachers to be "wishy-washy" and that exaggerated responses create a more favourable response.*'

Both examples refer to deliberate exaggeration, teachers and themselves becoming larger than life, yourself only more so: hyperself. They offer partial echoes of the conundrum presented at the start of this chapter: 'I try always to be myself: I have no one else to be'. They allow for the possibility that teaching is being yourself and acting at the same time. The student teacher offering the second response says 'exaggerated responses create a more favourable response'. Maybe good teachers find this hyperself, but if they do it must be a hard position to find, because other student teachers are aware that pupils are quick to identify falseness:

> '*You have to be yourself. Children are too streetwise and will catch you out – then you lose any respect. I speak from experience as a mother!*'

'I think I am myself when I teach, I find if the pupils see you as a "real" person with a normal life they respect you.'

It's now a little clearer where the effort implicit in 'I try always to be myself' comes from.

Self as a teaching resource

The responses of these student teachers introduce the possibility that when we teach and learn to teach we start to identify our own attributes carefully and use them quite deliberately – as if we become our own toolbox. Like a penknife we may have the potential to work in many ways, but often remain closed-up, some gadgets never employed until necessity calls them into use. These comments make clear how some student teachers become very conscious of the way they exploit particular aspects of their personality when teaching:

'You learn to play on certain things such as confidence and enthusiasm, and hide others such as weaknesses in knowledge and nervousness ...'

'You quickly learn to hide certain things, mannerisms. You also exaggerate certain parts of your personality, so that you can build relationships with your pupils. Occasionally you have to not be yourself in order to fulfil the teacher role, you have to try not to laugh at certain things pupils may do and learn to respond like a "teacher" even if you are not bothered by them wearing earrings for example ...'

'I think you have to be yourself to a degree when you teach – otherwise they find you out. It is also important to think about the "self" that you want to portray and how students will see this version of you. Pupils like to know about you, and the odd snippet goes a long way.'

In that last example, even the odd, apparently throwaway comment becomes strategic as the student teacher tries to manipulate how pupils perceive him. Interestingly, this sense of deliberateness comes through even in the comments of those who seem to deny it in considering themselves 'natural' as teachers, particularly when they use vocabulary such as 'tools' and 'techniques' to describe what they do:

'I think that I am myself when I teach, I have been told that I am a very calming effect on some classes! I try very hard to be myself. I am not a theatrical person, unlike my mentor from placement B, who leaps and jumps about at every opportunity. I try to lighten the situation by humour, which I have found it to be a very useful tool in most situations!'

'Surprisingly I feel I am very much "myself" when I teach. On the occasions that I needed to be anything other than myself I felt uncomfortable. I couldn't be "someone else" for a long period of time – it would be unrewarding and frustrating. Personally, I use theatrical techniques and drama to add pace and interest to lessons.'

That the self is a resource to be manipulated at will is especially evident in these two comments:

'It is important that you are able to switch and play another character when necessary.'

'I am very much myself when I teach – but have understood the different masks I must/am able to wear at the turn of a key!'

Both describe conscious choices made in response to a moment's necessity.

A professional version of myself

In commenting on their experiences of learning to teach, many student teachers remarked on how they felt they related to the institutions they found themselves in. Several refer to 'professional behaviour', one going as far as to identify 'a professional version of myself'. Sometimes an awareness of your professional self derives from specific responses to you offered by pupils. In this first instance, the response is closely tied to pupils' idea of what a given subject (in this instance Religious Education) is concerned with, and by extension the sort of person that might teach it:

'It's strange because my pupils expected a deeply religious Christian who was going to convert them. I'm actually religious, but also like drinking and gambling; I think this came out at

stages even though most of the time I was on guard to come across as a responsible role model.'

In considering the extent to which he was himself when he taught, one student teacher made a case for the necessity of also having 'a professional version':

'[I am myself] ... in terms of my social relationships to pupils, but this can challenge discipline. There needs to be a fine line between who you are as a person and who you are as a teacher.'

The 'fine line' may be drawn as part of institutional rules and regulations:

'I try to remain natural although I do feel obliged to reprimand students for petty things due to the school's specific policy, i.e. uniform ...'

Sometimes such a 'professional version' feels compelled to hide very personal concerns and worries, but in a way that further complicates the extent to which we can ever be true or genuine selves when we teach:

'I try to be myself as much as possible. Obviously, I remain professional but I've found that pupils respond much better to you if they feel you're being genuine with them. This is also effective in discipline strategies – pupils respect you and if they like you, are far more co-operative. Be fair to the pupils – this means being consistent because they need to know where they stand – even if you're having a "I'm fat; I hate myself" day – smile through it for the kids' sake ...'

The 'fine line' can thus be taut, fragile though it may be.

Why are you shouting? You're not at school now!

Our identities are probably shaped to some degree by the people around us, especially those who have known us a long time, and those who see us in off-guard moments. This section moves away from that first question, to provide student teacher responses to a different prompt – to comment on how family members and friends responded to them through the length of the preparation course.

When you learn to teach, the remarks of friends, families and partners can be quite telling. They'll maybe notice things about you that you don't, given that you're so wrapped up in the preparation process. Sometimes their comments may be wry, amusing – maybe you do something they perceive to be 'teacherly' that would never have drawn comment before. On other occasions, their observations might have very serious implications. Maybe they're trying to tell you something about your attitude to work, that maybe you haven't kept aside enough time for yourself? Though the process of learning to teach is one that makes huge demands on your time and energy, it is important that you strike a balance and find time for yourself. This balance will become ever more important as you take on further teaching responsibilities and make progress in your career. The comments that follow will give you some idea of what learning to teach looks like to those outside the process.

The student teachers who commented on the way other people talked about them during training often mentioned remarks made about their behaviour, as if 'teacherliness' was seeping into their very being and affecting the way they talked to their nearest and dearest. Parents 'told me not to talk to them like school children', and one student teacher's husband said 'Sometimes I talk to him like a teacher'. Often this wasn't just about the actual words used, but the manner in which student teachers spoke:

> *'They have sometimes commented on how I now use "teacher-ish" comments and looks when talking to them or when they are doing something they shouldn't!'*

One student teacher remarked that his 'teacher voice scares them', but that his 'teacher pose annoys them'. It's interesting to think about when such behaviour might come to light. Do you suddenly become more assertive when you learn to teach, bossing staff around in shops or insisting that friends pronounce their 'h's properly? Some responses showed that student teachers had been told they had developed a 'teacher stare', often used in connection with a certain tone of voice alluded to here:

> *'Mum, why are you shouting? You're not at school now!'*

'I went away with the Guides the other week and started talking like a teacher, which was quite odd.'

'I told a child off in the street once and my friend fell about laughing at my "teacher's voice"! People who knew me before know that I have become more serious about my own life, as this is the first time I have been truly responsible for other people, and this has changed me. Those who did not know me before seem to think I am incredibly capable and calm, which is a view of me that would make my old friends laugh!'

So much seems to be tied up with being able to use your voice differently. In the example just given, the student teacher seems to identify some sort of watershed, as if learning to teach has helped her reappraise herself, her whole life. When she mentions the possibility that her 'old friends' would laugh at the way new colleagues and peers now view her, she's touching on an experience that many of us may have when we begin teaching. Perhaps it does bring certain qualities to the fore, and maybe as you challenge your own expectations of yourself, the expectations others have of you inevitably have to change too. Obviously this is confusing to the people closest to you, and possibly a little disconcerting – 'My boyfriend says that I have become extremely grumpy!' One student teacher was accused of 'using a "teacher's voice" when arguing with my girlfriend'. With the example that follows, it could be interesting to think about how you would view this Biology student teacher before you start teaching, and how you might view her as you come to the end of an initial course:

'They have commented that I am always on the lookout for resources to use in class. While out shopping I had a great conversation with a member of the invertebrate society because I wanted to get some resources. How sad am I?'

The boundaries of what you regard as sane behaviour may shift slightly, to a position somewhat off-kilter with those maintained by your non-teaching kith and kin. Sometimes this relates back to comments many entrants to the profession must have heard – 'that I'm mad for going into secondary teaching' – but sometimes it might relate to a difficulty friends and family can have in recognising the pressures teaching places on you, and the way it can occupy you thoughts so constantly. Student teachers variously described how family had observed that they 'looked tired', 'growly', 'stressed', how they might exclaim 'you're not doing more work?!' Friends and family also noted 'my social life has declined', 'that I work too hard, have no life, and spend every breathing waking moment lesson planning, marking etc.'. Maybe it's because 'many family members cannot understand what motivates me to do this job', but equally the comments you've just read indicate that your behaviour as a student teacher could cause concern to those close to you. The intensity of teaching will no doubt diminish the time you have to spend with them. One student had been described as 'grey, thin, pale and worn-out', while family members of another felt he had spent a lot of time 'in solitary'. All these comments suggest that for the people looking in, being a teacher can mean looking busy, stretched, and even a little isolated.

Fortunately, the same people can see the immense benefits of being a teacher and the significant positive impact it can have on those involved. Many student teachers reported being described as far more confident and organised ('people have teased me about my post-its'), but also as being 'more relaxed in my bearing'. Many wrote of the compliments they had received, where friends and family seem to have recognised how through teaching others they have fulfilled their potential. For one student this involved them making clear 'that I have become stronger – teaching empowers me, I give a lot more praise and encouragement to friends'; for another it was a recognition of 'how hard I have worked and how I have committed myself to the course'. Sometimes praise was tied to acknowledgement of some transformation: 'a future trainee teacher was shocked when I said I was a quiet, shy type of person – no one would have disputed this before the course.'

Just as important was the way friends and family noticed how 'happy' these new teachers had become, noticing student teachers becoming 'content' and 'settled', their pleasure in teaching visible: 'They are pleased to see me doing something that I naturally enjoy'. These encouraging remarks are best drawn to an end with two more compliments. Both indicate that as far as close acquaintances see it, these student teachers have finally become teachers. The first is short, but possibly the ultimate compliment: 'They wish their kids were pupils at my school.' The second is 'you'll make a fantastic teacher', which is significant because of what came with it: the student teacher's sense that 'the reality of the craft and skills needed to achieve this is so very different from your "nature"'.

Life lessons

It would be artificial to pull together the comments you've read here to find general patterns, when a basic premise of the chapter has been that learning to teach feels different for everyone. There is, however, one idea I do want to mention. Whether or not you see teaching as an 'act', it can shape and influence who you are as much as your own identity shapes how you teach. It's a notion best expressed by this student teacher, and stands as an apt conclusion to the main body of this book:

> 'I have always enjoyed having a "stage" to perform on – being the centre of attention. This comes out in my teaching – expositions run on and I can monopolise the airwaves! This is not effective all the time, though. What I learn in the classroom compliments those other "life lessons". What I'm saying is that learning to teach effectively and developing as an individual is a cyclical process. You understand!?'

Chapter 10

Learning from experience

Jeff Battersby

This concluding chapter draws together the plethora of advice from student teachers, tutors and mentors from the richness of the training experiences they have enjoyed, lived through or witnessed. It is clear that while learning to teach, learning from of observation of established teachers and working alongside other colleagues or students can inform your preparation and challenge your thinking about your role in the learning process along the way. Through these experiences you will gain a clearer understanding about teaching, about your subject and the whole curriculum, about the pupils and about yourself.

So having digested the details of these reflections of newly emerging teachers about their experiences during their training, do you see parallels in your own experience and training? Hopefully you are reassured rather than despondent, able to recognise the gradual growth, maturing and evolution of the fledgling teachers as they embark on their journey into the profession. Are there questions that you need to ask yourself or your tutors and mentors in school about the range of experiences reported? Are you having the same or are you missing out?

It is clear from the observations made by these student teachers, and doubtless you and your peers, that everyone who we meet and work with seems to know what teaching is all about, not least because of their experiences as pupils in the system. The majority of people appear able to recognise the characteristics of a good teacher, the person who inspired them to learn. These are the teachers who lit the fires of their imaginations, nurtured their fragile confidence, empowered and enabled them to become successful learners. These are the teachers who are celebrated in the weekly 'My best teacher' feature in the *Times Educational Supplement*. By the same token, we all appear able to recognise teachers who have fallen short in our expectations. For some student teachers there is a desire to 'right the wrongs' of their experience, to offer their pupils a 'better deal' than they had as pupils. The same is true when it comes to perceptions of the most appropriate strategies and approaches for successful teaching and learning, most often from the position of 'it worked for me, so I'll adopt it', or 'it didn't so I won't, because it will not work'.

How far are the reasons why you chose to train to become a teacher paralleled by those of these student teachers? Was it your passion and enthusiasm for your specialist subject which you wanted to continue exploring and to share with the next generations of learners? Was it the desire to be involved in encouraging the enthusiasm of the young to acquire all those new facts, skills and ideas, to foster a love for learning? Do you see yourself as a teacher of your specialist subject or a teacher of pupils? Are you putting teaching or learning to the forefront? Have your initial thoughts changed with some first-hand observation and experience?

Whilst the feeling might not be a constant one either during your training or even when fully inducted into the profession, the sentiment expressed by one student teacher that:

> *'I'm absolutely loving being a teacher, it keeps putting a smile on my face,'*

is one which is more frequently felt than not, and anyway sleepless nights are better spent creating learning objectives than counting sheep!

A key message emerging when learning about teaching in the early stages is to accept your deficiencies and inefficiencies and acknowledge that you are unlikely to produce perfect lessons which will inspire and enthuse absolutely all of the pupils in the class – well, not on every occasion! It is important to identify the challenges of lesson planning, preparation of resources, classroom management, assessment and the administrative tasks associated with each of these key components of teaching and learning. You will realise very quickly the enormous workload you are taking on and that your inexperience will mean that those lesson plans do 'take hours', especially in the early stages. It is all too easy to become disheartened and demoralised in this situation, especially if you haven't made significant gains and apparent progress whilst on placement in a school. It's a case of gritting your teeth and seeking reassurance from your mentors on the small achievements you have made. Another guarantee is that you can 'expect the unexpected' during your training and throughout your career in teaching. Your life is never going to be dull in the classroom, and hopefully it won't be for your pupils either.

The plethora of advice alluded to earlier is ample and is available from tutors, mentors, peers and even the pupils as you begin to learn about teaching. Teaching and learning are dynamic, and you will realise very quickly that you cannot guarantee that by structuring your lesson and tasks for one class, these will work as effectively with another: if only it were the case! Equally, you will also realise that by adopting the same teaching styles and strategies as your mentor or other class teachers you observe, you might not achieve quite the same level of engagement in and enthusiasm for learning from the pupils. You cannot be the exact replica of your mentor or other teachers, as John Gordon illustrates in the chapter about 'Learning about yourself'.

Experienced teachers are clearly more experienced and have honed their teaching skills to a greater extent than you have been able to do at this early stage of your career. They have usually developed well-established relationships with the pupils who know and understand the expectations that the teacher has of them when being taught in their lessons. Student teachers, however, are helped by the ethos and expectations that the school has of the pupils. The systems and procedures, the frameworks that Terry Haydn describes, are important to know and to ensure that they are adhered to, by you as a trainee as well as the pupils. In so doing you gain strength and support from adopting the mantle or status of the teacher and all that goes with this title. Student teachers state that they can only 'be themselves' in the classroom, though they begin to recognise how they strengthen certain of their attributes and downplay others. They 'switch characters', 'wear different masks' as they learn how to engage pupils in learning. It is anything but an exact science.

Time management is crucial for both your time in the classroom as well as outside it. Most of the student teachers allude to the need to have a crash course in being a professional and making every minute count. This is imperative when planning the lesson to be taught and for the pupils to engage in. The best advice is to try to visualise the lesson from the pupils' perspective as well as yours as the teacher. What are the pupils doing when you are talking to them? How will you explain the complexity of the key idea you are trying to get across and how will you know whether the pupils have understood it? What questions will you ask to ascertain this, of whom, and what answer will you expect in response? How will you ensure that the gifted and talented amongst the class are stretched in their thinking, whilst those least able to grasp the complexity of the idea are not left floundering?

Student teachers and even experienced teachers know through experience that it is one thing knowing what to do, quite another actually carrying it out, especially when the pupils haven't read the script. Key messages emerge from your body language and the level of confidence you have in managing the pupils and their learning. This is most apparent when asking pupils questions. It's easy for you because you know the question you have asked, and presumably you know the answer too. But put yourself in the pupils' shoes and consider for a moment what they hear when you ask a question. They need to consider the question as it is asked, or as they perceive it. This might be different to your perception because of the language and phrasing of the question and the complexity of the ideas involved which they need to respond to. Coupled with this is the level of confidence that the individual pupil has in knowing the answer to the question, being able to articulate it in front of his or her peers and whether it is worth the risk in doing so. We all need thinking and response time when being asked questions, even if this is only a split-second, but it can be interpreted by the novice teacher that the pupils are either unable or unwilling to respond, that there is a mutiny afoot! In this scenario it is all too easy to ask another question or rephrase the original question, but put a different twist or emphasis on it so it appears different, if only subtly so. The whole scenario is played out again, which can become demoralising for both teacher and pupils alike. It's OK to have a silence and a delay in the pupils' responses to your questions – well, seconds yes, but minutes no!

In situations such as this take responsibility for your actions and the questions you ask. If a sea of 'blank faces' greets you, or if the responses are inappropriate, then take the question back, own up to the fact that you have probably not phrased it appropriately, or asked the wrong question and try again, but this time with a different question. You will not lose face with the pupils this way and they certainly won't have done so as you have reprieved them individually or collectively from a potentially negative situation. They will warm to you as a result, as long as you learn from this and start to use appropriate language and offer them opportunities where they can express their knowledge, understanding and skills successfully.

Tutors and mentors put great emphasis on self-reflection and evaluation of the teaching and learning that has – or has not – occurred in the lesson. Student teachers have identified throughout this book that they have learnt more from situations which have been taxing and from 'failing' experiences than from those lessons which appear to lack key incidents. It is important for you to identify the things which went well from your point of view, as well as from the pupils', and to try to understand why. It is through this evaluation and reflection that positive, effective strategies and procedures can be reused and incorporated in your armoury for use on other occasions. Despite listening to advice from all quarters and knowing what to do, mistakes are inevitable. These are crucial for your development as a teacher and for your understanding of what makes for good teaching and learning. Reassurance from your mentor will build your confidence as you begin to recognise and acknowledge your emerging achievements and strengths.

In the early stages of your teaching it is usual for you to be more concerned about the delivery of the subject content than perhaps pupils' engagement and enjoyment of their learning. You will prepare for a lesson with either greater or lesser confidence depending on the subject matter to be taught. In situations where you feel secure in your subject knowledge you will appear more confident as you prepare for the lesson as well as when you are in front of the pupils delivering the lesson. Where the converse is true, then seeds of doubt are sown. The challenges here are evident from the gaps you and your tutors have identified through your subject knowledge audits, but it will also be manifested by your inability to answer some questions asked of you by the pupils. There are only so many times when you can 'pass' or ask to 'phone a friend' to stall the situation before the pupils and your mentor begin to have concerns and lose confidence in you. Offering opportunities for the pupils to 'find out for the next lesson' will encourage some to do so in an effort to impress you, to be one up on you or because you have enthused and interested them. In the same way that you are not necessarily aware of your lack of specific knowledge and understanding of the subject, the same is true with your pupils. Your challenge is to develop this subject knowledge with them to enable them to become more capable mathematicians, scientists, geographers or musicians.

Confidence in subject knowledge looms large for all trainees, and many concur how they were only able to 'relax' once they had acquired an understanding of the basic concepts that were to be taught. This is particularly true when teaching a second subject and is a more common feeling expressed by Science trainees who are obliged to teach all three of the sciences. The majority of student teachers wished to appear to have 'expert knowledge' so that they would be able to impress their pupils, and consequently pupils would have greater confidence in them as teachers. Developing greater subject knowledge makes lesson planning easier too, as you become aware of the logical steps of progression from simple to more complex ideas within the subject and think more carefully about how the pupils might access these through a range of learning activities.

However – and there always is a however – a sound knowledge of the subject does not always correlate with an ability to teach it, nor even to be able to split the subject into 'bite-sized chunks' for the pupils. If only it were this straightforward! Knowing or not knowing the subject matter is one thing, but trying to make it interesting and engaging for the pupils is another. Again, it's easier to interest and engage those who are 'switched on' to learning and to the subject, but something more challenging to interest, engage and enthuse the disaffected and disinterested pupil. However, tutors, mentors and trainees alike identify that planning lessons and identifying learning objectives give insights into the subject, and an additional appreciation of how to develop and employ knowledge for a specific purpose. It also enables the development of a clear conceptual framework to be able to organise learning based on existing pupil knowledge and that which is to be learnt.

So how will you become the subject expert and develop your subject knowledge? To misquote Donald Rumsfeld: there are some areas of your subject that you know that you know and others that you know you don't know, but what about those areas that you don't know you don't know and how will you know that you don't know these? In Chapter 3, Nalini Boodhoo stresses the importance of pre-course audits to augment a needs analysis and identify tasks which can begin to address those identified gaps in your subject knowledge before the course begins in earnest. Ongoing audits are extremely useful checks on areas of weakness or concern as well as being a helpful reassurance that gaps are indeed being filled as you tackle those areas of the subject you had long forgotten, chose not to study in the past or didn't know existed!

Some trainees put themselves through the mill by tackling GCSE and A-level exam papers to check their subject knowledge, though this is probably better done away from the pupils rather than in front of them in case there are some embarrassing lapses and distinct canyons, let alone gaps, in subject knowledge. Taking the opportunity to join post-16 classes to reacquaint themselves with the subject as well as observe teaching approaches with this age group is a useful strategy to adopt to combine learning about the subject at the same time as learning how to teach it. Some mentors ask trainees to teach aspects of their subject knowledge which is a perceived area of weakness. Student teachers testify that whilst this causes some initial angst, it does 'focus the mind' and invariably leads to successful teaching on their part as well as successful learning on the part of the pupils.

Knowledge is in a continuous state of change and development in all subjects. New research sometimes challenges the theoretical underpinnings of the subject, new texts and illustrative examples become available, as in the case of geographical phenomena, which requires student teachers to acquire this new knowledge and be confident in using it prior to introducing it into their lessons or when assessing pupils' knowledge of the subject. Peers can be an invaluable resource as you tap into the expertise of your training cohort to gain insights and understanding of the subject of which you were unaware. They are often a useful sounding board too, as well as a source of knowledge of those areas of the subject you are unsure of. Equally pupils bring knowledge to the lessons, and the skill of the teacher is to coax this from them for the mutual benefit of all. Knowledge drawn from pupils in this way raises their self-belief and their confidence in you as their teacher as well as in their own capability in learning about the subject with you.

Another significant challenge is identified by many student teachers relating to the teaching of subjects. It is one thing to convey information about the subject to pupils, but quite another to make it meaningful to them. This is where a clear conceptual framework of the subject is vitally important alongside an ability to organise pupils' learning, which is itself based on your knowledge of their existing knowledge and understanding of the subject. You also need to be aware of the ethical dimensions of the subject and the values and attitudes underpinning it. You will need to be conscious of your own values, confident and comfortable with them before you begin to engage with those held by the pupils. This can pose another interesting dimension of teaching the subject. Student teachers have indicated that it is important to make the subject relevant and to relate to pupils' real lived worlds, choosing examples and case studies which they can empathise with, which excite them and move them.

'My best teacher', which appears as a regular feature in the *Times Educational Supplement*, invariably highlights the quality of the relationship that the teacher has forged with the pupils as well as the enthusiasm and inspiration demonstrated by the teacher in the classroom. So who are these inspirational teachers and how do they execute their talents to enable, encourage and engage so enthusiastically with the pupils and with their subject? Chapter 4 outlines ways of finding out through focussed observation of these teachers at work to gain insights into the way in which teachers develop positive relationships with their classes, making adjustments to meet the needs of individual pupils, situations and circumstances. These appear instinctive but have been honed through experience and reflection. This is particularly evident when considering classroom management and discipline, knowing how to react to and respond to different pupils and situations, being decisive, firm, fair and consistent yet being inconsistent too, depending on the specific circumstances and pupil. Learning to ensure that pupils are given a choice of action and reaction is crucial, rather than an ultimatum which boxes you and the pupil into a corner with only 'Hobson's choice' available to each of you. How do these good teachers manage that?

Through the keen, well-trained eye and ear you will pick up on the key phrases used in these trying moments, the options available, targets set, and learn that good classroom management is as much about the way you behave as it is about how the pupils behave. Your body language, hand gestures and eye contact are as important as the phrases, language and volume you use when encouraging, praising, admonishing or conveying messages to the pupils. You will notice that good teachers act as if they expect things to happen and their pupils to respond to their direction. Your success in the classroom and with the pupils will be determined by how easily you are able to adopt the roles and responsibilities of the teacher and 'act as if' your pupils will respond to you and do as you ask of them – well, most of the time! There will be occasions when you get it wrong and give instructions which do not make sense or are impossible to carry out and the pupils see through the mixed messages you are giving. It's back to the language and phrasing again, so, as before, make sure your brain is engaged before you put your mouth into gear!

Student teachers offer useful tips and insights which emphasise how they have learnt from observing successful teachers and successful lessons. They report how it is important to keep calm, nail problems early and wander around the classroom rather than being rooted at the front or trying to hide behind the teacher's desk. Further insights are gained from detailed reflection on student teachers' own teaching and lessons, which is key to their continued professional development and greater success in the classroom and with the pupils. It was also noted by many student teachers that opportunities to observe other teachers, both in and outside of their own specialism, was of great value once they had gained some experience teaching for themselves. This was even more valuable towards the end of the course when they had become accomplished teachers in their own right, having met all the Standards for QTS. Further reflection and discussion of a greater range of teaching and learning strategies enabled them to consider how they might incorporate those into their own teaching before the end of the course or adding to their knowledge bank as they moved towards their first teaching post.

To a large extent your learning about teaching is developed when working with or alongside other teachers who are the key people in your training, especially your mentor. You will not be expected to launch into a full teaching commitment from day one of your training, but rather be eased in gently. The training programme provides opportunities for you to work with and alongside individual pupils and small groups of pupils before you embark on whole-class teaching. There is a gradual increase in responsibility for classes, which occurs during periods of serial and block placement. You will find that you will have opportunities to take short episodes or periods of a lesson working alongside the class teacher. You might introduce the lesson, introduce a specific task once the teacher has started the lesson or be responsible for the plenary session, where you ascertain from the pupils the key areas of learning that had occurred in the lesson.

Team-teaching should be a safe environment to work in initially, if not throughout your training, as the class teacher or mentor has responsibility for pupils' learning and all aspects of classroom management. This provides opportunities for a smooth transition in responsibility from the class teacher to you. This is also more effective if you have been involved in the joint planning of the lessons and agreeing the learning objectives.

Some tensions can arise if the class teacher 'fails to notice' or 'appears to ignore' poor behaviour from some of the pupils, yet you are aware of it. Where does the responsibility lie? What should your response be to this when it is not your lesson? How do you inform the teacher that they might have missed or misjudged a pupil? How do you ensure that the pupil is aware that you are aware of their indiscretions? As a teacher working alongside another, you have to exercise tact and diplomacy and not undermine the authority of the class teacher whilst at the same time uphold the standards and expectations of the school. You have to act as a professional at all times, especially as your mentor is key to your development and in the assessment of your capability.

Working alongside different colleagues is an important part of your training and the job. Student teachers refer to problems they have encountered when trying to please different teachers and be seen to be acting on what appears at times to be conflicting advice. As Roy Barton explains in Chapter 6, most mentors are aware of this 'problem' and want to develop an open debate and dialogue with their student teacher to discuss issues of teaching and class management. It is all right to have a view and to express it, but equally, you need to be able to take and act upon advice given to you. Mentors encourage student teachers to be 'open and honest' in discussing problems experienced in class and to 'voice fears'. This is crucial for your development and in being able to make greater sense of issues related to teaching and learning. This also helps both you and your mentor to set Specific, Measurable, Achievable, Realistic and Time-related (SMART) targets for you to enable you to progress towards achieving the Standards and for your continued development.

Earlier, I asked whether you see yourself as a teacher of your subject or as a teacher of children. Whilst this is not a simplistic 'either, or', it is being aware of 'the hidden curriculum' which will determine the kind of teacher you are or will become. You will be well aware already of the various roles and responsibilities which teachers take on and how well you fit with these. There are high expectations of you as a role model for your pupils as you demonstrate and promote the positive values, attitudes and behaviours that you expect from your pupils. Marian Agombar draws attention in Chapter 7 to the importance that the government has put on the 'curriculum' in promoting the spiritual, moral, social, cultural, physical and mental development and the well-being of the individual as well as in preparing pupils for the opportunities, responsibilities and experiences of adult life. In order to fulfil these aims it is incumbent on us all to play our part in ensuring that this occurs.

Through your teaching you will be able to find opportunities to enable pupils to recognise, reaffirm or rethink their own values and attitudes to issues such as discrimination, prejudice, stereotyping, justice and truth as you deal with topics such as the Holocaust, 9/11, slavery, terrorism, child abuse, female circumcision, binge drinking, being a vegetarian, body ornamentation, cloning, closure of the local post office, and second homes. Essentially what is your position on sex, drugs and rock 'n' roll and, of course, school uniform? Pupils want to know where you stand on these issues and whether you live your life according to a specific moral code.

Your attitude to your pupils, the way that you treat them and deal with them and their issues, in and outside the classroom, will demonstrate your values and your respect for their social, cultural, religious and ethnic backgrounds as well as those of their parents. This can become more challenging when it is clear that the values, beliefs and expectations of some of your pupils and parents differ significantly from your own. With the onset of the 'Every Child Matters' agenda, teachers have a significant role to play in association with other agencies to ensure that children are able to be healthy, stay safe, enjoy and achieve, make a positive contribution and achieve economic well-being. You need to be aware of the specific roles and responsibilities you have 'in loco parentis' as a teacher.

Many student teachers saw their role acting as a form tutor as the richest experience when in school, saw the potentially great impact that they could have on pupils' lives, though many pupils didn't want to know or thank you for your concern. At times this part of the job was 'like walking on eggshells'. This role and its associated responsibilities also shocked some student teachers as they discovered insights into worlds that they had never experienced themselves, nor wished to. They were uncomfortable with some disclosures made by pupils and at a loss to find an appropriate response to some of the problems being experienced.

Being vulnerable comes with the territory of being a student teacher as pupils try to find out your personal details, develop a 'crush' on you, make suggestive or derogatory remarks. This can either undermine or boost your self-confidence and your authority. It is important that you share any concerns and worries emanating from such comments with your mentor, professional tutor and university or college tutor. They will be in a position to offer advice or take action which will relieve the situation, as with Marian's trainee in Chapter 7 who was made to feel uncomfortable by a pupil.

Terry Haydn explains in Chapter 8 how all teachers operate within constraining frameworks relating to professional conduct, the taught curriculum, the organisation and management of schools amongst others which have to be understood and adhered to by student teachers also as they strive to attain the Standards for qualified teacher status. Teachers value opportunities for professional autonomy, to be original, creative and do different from others, developing the curriculum and their teaching and learning strategies which appeal to and engage the pupils whilst still operating within the constraints imposed by the National Curriculum or public examination specifications. Student teachers are introduced to and become aware of a wide range of strategies on their course and are encouraged to use their initiative when in school. However, they do so as long as they stay within the bounds agreed with their mentor, the department or the head teacher. There is only so much freedom a mentor can give to a trainee if they are to have a constructive and positive working relationship.

Mentors will encourage student teachers to try different ideas, strategies and approaches to teaching and learning to develop their experience, confidence and expertise, safe in the knowledge that there is a 'safe pair of hands' ready to support them should things go 'pear-shaped'. It is important to experiment whilst on placement and during your training so that you have considered the advantages and disadvantages, the problems and the pitfalls of some of these prior to your first appointment as a newly qualified teacher, when 'disasters' could taint your year. On placement the responsibility for the class lies with the designated class teacher, so you can safely experiment and should things go wrong your mentor can take over again and rectify the problems. Just don't do this too often though, as you do need to demonstrate that you can achieve the standards and prove yourself capable as a new teacher.

One of the most important lessons to be learnt is that teachers are part of a team or several teams and it is vital that you operate effectively and consistently within the teams you are in. As Terry highlights, the key questions asked of and about student teachers are: Would I like this person teaching my own kids? Would they be a good person to have in the department/school? Would they be a good colleague? Answers to each of these are found through the observation and experience that mentors and others gain whilst working with the student teacher, from the evidence of the way that the student teacher operates through their situational understanding and their actions in relation to pupils, in classrooms and with colleagues.

Understanding the complexity of the extensive range of competencies which have to be demonstrated by a student teacher in order to become an accomplished teacher is one of the most difficult and challenging tasks confronting the would-be teacher. It is how you manage to realise these and demonstrate effectiveness in your teaching, classroom management and in your professionalism that will carry you through to a successful conclusion at the end of your training with a recommendation that you be given qualified teacher status (QTS). Along the way you should work within the constraining frameworks to make small gains against the standards as you yo-yo between the 'hopeless' and the 'brilliant' on the same day and even with the same class in the same lesson. Teaching can certainly be a roller-coaster of a job!

Throughout your training and throughout your career you will realise very quickly that teaching is an emotional business. In Chapter 9, John Gordon tells of the conflicts that student teachers wrestle with in coming to terms with their self-belief, their doubts, the constantly changing persona to fit different situations. They are considering what it feels like to learn to teach, how it affects them, how they perceive themselves and how others think of them, notably their colleagues and their pupils. Developing self-belief is key to developing as a teacher and the finding of your self will mean that you are no longer self-conscious. It is only then that you will be able to become the larger-than-life character that is often needed in the classroom. Do you remember those teachers from your school experience? Were they the ones who inspired and enthused you? However, student teachers also tell how pupils see through the fake persona very quickly and how they can suffer as a result. No doubt you have memories of less successful teachers yourself, who didn't engage with you or your peers. Successful student teachers have been able to identify their attributes and use them deliberately, as one student teacher states, being 'like a Swiss army knife' only employing some of gadgets when necessary and appropriate.

In a similar way, student teachers who are able to wear different masks and present themselves in different guises are more likely to engage with their pupils. They also realise that they have to remain as the role model for their pupils, being the professional adopting the mantle of the teacher. However, they also note how friends and family are quick to chastise them when adopting the teacher role, voice and pose outside of school, especially if this persona has not been seen before. The most telling piece of advice is to be yourself and be true to yourself, but be able to make some changes to yourself as the need arises so that you become that successful teacher you intend to be.

Here's to a successful training year and career in teaching for you. We all hope that you will 'absolutely love being a teacher' and that teaching will indeed put a smile on your face. It is important to remember that pupils enjoy learning through the smiling eyes of their teachers, through their energy, enthusiasm and commitment. Whatever you teach, you need to teach pupils to love learning. You have the opportunity and privilege to do this and to bring distinction to each and every one of the pupils you teach. That is some challenge. Are you up for it? We and your pupils hope that you are, and expect so too.

References

Aldrich, R. (2002) *The Institute of Education, 1902–2002: A Centenary History*. London: Institute of Education.

Ausubel, D. (1968) *Educational Psychology: A Cognitive View*. New York: Holt, Rinehart and Winston.

Capel, S. Leask, M. and Turner, T. (1999) *Learning to Teach in the Secondary School*. London: Routledge.

Cockburn, A. and Haydn, T. (2004) *Recruiting and Retaining Teachers: Understanding Why Teachers Teach*. London: RoutledgeFalmer.

Cockburn, A., Haydn, T. and Oliver, A. (2000) 'Why not teaching?' Paper presented to the British Pyschological Society, December 2000.

DfEE (2000) *The National Curriculum*. London: DfEE.

DfES (2002) *Qualifying to Teach*. London: DfES/TTA.

Elliott, J. (1991) *Action Research for Educational Change*. Buckingham: Open University Press.

Evans, K. (2002) *Negotiating the Self: Identity, Sexuality, and Emotion in Learning to Teach*. London and New York: RoutledgeFalmer

Haydn, T. (2001) 'From a very peculiar department to a very successful school: Transference issues arising out of a study of an improving school', *School Leadership and Management*, 21 (4): 415–39.

Hutchings, M., Menter, I., Ross, A. and Thomson, D. (2002) 'Teacher supply and retention in London: Key findings and implications from a study of six boroughs in 1998–99', in I. Menter, M. Hutchings and A. Ross (eds), *The Crisis in Teacher Supply*. Stoke-on-Trent: Trentham, pp. 175–206.

Klemp, G. (1977) *Three Factors of Success in the World of Work: Implications for Curriculum in Higher Education*. Boston, MA: McBer.

Kyriacou, C. (1995) *Essential Teaching Skills*. Cheltenham: Stanley Thornes.

Kyriacou, C. and Coulthard, M. (2000) 'Undergraduates' views of teaching as a career choice', *Journal of Education for Teaching*, 26 (2): 117–26.

Millett, A. (1998) Quoted in *Times Educational Supplement*, 22 May.

Moon, B. and Mayes, A.S. (eds) (1994) *Teaching and Learning in the Secondary School*. Milton Keynes: Open University.

Priyadharshini, E. and Robinson-Pant, A. (2003) 'The attractions of teaching: An investigation into why people change careers to teach', *Journal of Education for Teaching*, 29 (3): 95–112.

Scott Baumann, A., Bloomfield, A. and Roughton, L. (1997) *Becoming a Secondary School Teacher*. London: Hodder & Stoughton.

Spear, M., Gould, K. and Lee, B. (2000) *Who Would Be a Teacher? A Review of Factors Motivating snd Demotivating Prospective and Practising Teachers*. Slough: NFER.

Stenhouse, L. (1975) *An Introduction to Curriculum Research and Development*. London: Heinemann.

Taplin, K. (2001) 'Do the pupils I teach find physics more difficult than other areas within science?' Unpublished MA Dissertation, University of East Anglia.

Teacher Training Agency (2003) *Qualifying to Teach*. London: TTA Publication No. TPU1065/2p/20k/fmp/sep 03.

Wragg, E. (1994) *An Introduction to Classroom Observation*. London: Routledge.

Index

Note: page numbers in italics denote figures or tables

DATE DUE

LB 1707 .B38 2006

Battersby, Jeff.

Preparing to teach